Edward Walford

Patient Griselda, and Other Poems

Edward Walford

Patient Griselda, and Other Poems

ISBN/EAN: 9783744770965

Printed in Europe, USA, Canada, Australia, Japan

Cover: Foto ©Thomas Meinert / pixelio.de

More available books at **www.hansebooks.com**

INSCRIBED TO

A "BELOVED PHYSICIAN,'

J. G. SINCLAIR COGHILL, Esq

AS A TRIBUTE OF

GRATITUDE AND RESPECT.

———

" *Quod spiro et placeo,* **si** *placeo, tuum est.*"
—HORACE IV. OD. III., 24.

PREFACE TO THE FIRST EDITION.

If it be necessary in any case to write a "Preface" to a volume of "Poems," it seems doubly necessary in mine. I have lived to over seventy without giving way to the vice of *smoking*, and why then can I not be contented to abstain to my very end from the vice of *verse-making?* My apology is on this wise: I naturally wish to vindicate my good name when I am gone, and to leave behind me some permanent proofs that I have sought and striven in my humble sphere to justify the good lessons which I learned first at my mother's knee and subsequently at the Charter House, and above all, within the walls of Balliol College, Oxford, to which I owe any good that may be in me, and any success that I have achieved in life. It is in such of his writings as flow from his heart, and especially in his poetical effusions, that a man's character may be read; and I am not without a sort of secret hope that I may "stand well" with some at least of those who "read between the lines" of these verses.

Warned by a long and all but fatal illness, I am conscious that at seventy-two my end cannot be far off. As Wordsworth writes:

"Life's autumn past, I stand on winter's verge."

But meantime I believe that, after all, my more "Serious and Sentimental" poems, in spite of their faults, will appeal to the hearts of some at least of my readers. At all events, Miss Braddon, —who some twenty years ago, put "Griselda" on the stage at the Princess' Theatre, wrote to me at the time:

"I have read your 'Griselda' with much pleasure, and think you have "given a very charming version of the simple and, to my mind, most "pathetic old Story; and you have also drawn from the Legend an "admirable moral, which gives grace to the close of your poem."

The late Mr. William Longman, the eminent Author and Publisher, wrote to me under date Dec. 23, 1873:

"I think your 'Griselda' is *perfectly charming*, and my children will "all read it one after the other."

Mr. Longman told me afterwards that the reading of my lines had made him weep; and it is something to be proud of in after life to feel that one has moved a publisher to tears. The poem originally appeared in the *St. James' Magazine*; it was re-printed in "Gems of National Poetry," published by Warne; and by the Editor's permission I now reproduce it.

As to the rest of the contents of this little volume, especially of those in the second part, I would express myself in the words of Thackeray in his "Virginians," (ii., 12) "I dare say that what I have written is only taken out of books, or parodied from poems which I have read and imitated, like other men." But in no case have they been "written to order." As Miss Yonge says in *Heartsease*, "Pegasus won't let himself out on hire." Good or bad, my verses are genuine; and if they are very varied and inconsistent in tone, it is because at different periods of my life, my feelings have been very different. I lay little or no claim to originality; and I fear that many of the "Epigrams" in my second part are merely rhymed versions of anecdotes which I read, or heard from the lips of friends, many years ago. Such, however, as they are, I send them forth, regardless of the opinion of venal critics, but anxious *laudari a laudatis viris*.

E. WALFORD.

St. Boniface, Ventnor, October, 1894.

PREFACE TO THE SECOND EDITION.

The first Edition of these Poems, consisting of 250 copies, not having been sufficient to supply the orders sent by private friends, no portion of the impression reached the hands of the public. Accordingly a second issue of 250 copies has been printed, and any profits arising from the sale of the two Editions will be devoted partly to some one or other of the Charities of the Order of St. John, and partly to the Royal Hospital for Consumption at Ventnor.

E. WALFORD.

Ventnor, March, 1895.

CONTENTS.

PART I.

	PAGE.
Patient Griselda	1
Ghismonde the Fair	18
The Capuchin Convent	24
The Witches' Sabbath	32
The Maidens of Verdun	37
St. Elizabeth of Hungary	40
"Constance"	42
Friendship; An Idyll	48
Growth and Progress	50
Rienzi; A Dialogue	51
The Last Plantagenet	55
A Prophet Indeed	57
Shenstone and Cowper	58
The Queen's Jubilee Visit to the City	60
The Pilgrim's Death	60
My Library	62
Life's Harmony; Man and Woman	65
Beauty	65
Beppo; Stanzas for Music	66
To E. Bastard, of Kitley	67
To the Birds on Return of Spring	67
The Poet's Walk	68
Lines Suggested by W. S. Landor's Decameron	68
An Irish Eviction at Christmas	69
The House of Lords	72
Our New Premier, Lord Rosebery	73
The Curse of Meg Merrilies	74
"Three Acres and a Cow"	75
The Execution of Vaillant	76
"Perfect Peace"; Lines written in Illness	78
"Kyrie Eleïson"	78
The Gift of Tears	79
From An Old Ecclesiastical Poem	79
Nazareth	80
The Order of St. John	80
The Beatitudes Paraphrased	81
David Paraphrased	82
On the Death of a Beloved Sister	83
The Sleep of the Faithful Departed	84
To My Guardian Angel: Morning	85
To the Same: Evening	86
The Infancy of Jesus	86
Suffer the Little Children to come unto Me	88
The Holy Trinity	88
Home	90
A Thought on Creeds	91
Gems from Classic Mines	91—99

PART II.

	PAGE
"My Emma and Cupid"	101
"I've a Notion" (lines read before the "Odd Volumes")	102
The Lay of the Fat Boy in Pickwick	112
My New Arm Chair	114
"This is the Land of Australia"	116
To Lady Clare; Verba Novissima	119
St. Peter at the Gate of Heaven	126
An Omnium-Gatherum List	127
"Ellicott Skinflint"	130
Mons. Le Duc	132
Horace Paraphrased	135
A Distant Day; A Prophecy	137
Christmas; an "Acrostic"	137
To Miss ——	138
Recipe for a Novel, after G. P. R. James	138
To "E.M.P."	139
A Valentine	140
Another Valentine	141
"All Men are Liars"	142
A Homely Parody	143
On Receiving a Present of Game	143
To Jane, with a Violet	143
At Christmas-tide, by a Cynic	143
To Clara ——	144
Truth v. Lies	144
To My Alma Mater	144
The Decade Decayed	145
Dr. Watts' Libel on Dogs	146
A Times Advertisement and its Answer	146
My Piano and I	147

EPIGRAMS.

On H.H. Pope Leo XIII	148
In Memoriam Cardinal Manning	148
On an Eccentric Old Gentlemen	149
To an Attorney who offered me Advice Gratis	149
At the "Odd Volumes"	150
The Profit of being Late	150
A Three-bottle Man	151
"A Bee in his Bonnet"	151
Impromptu, on Carrying off a Hat	151
Sisters, with a Difference	151
On the Walford Arms and Crest	152
Composed near Snowdon	153
Marriage; a Reply	153
A Puritan Defined	153
Christmas Fools	153
The Dying Poacher	154

CONTENTS.

	PAGE
On a Robber on a Gibbet ..Sham Strawberry Leaves	154
The Fifth Commandment; New Version	154
A Threatened Clearance ..	155
Legge v. Yates; a Libel Case	155
On Charles Bradlaugh, M.P.	155
Land and Water	156
To Mrs. ———— on the death of her Fox Terrier	156
On My Dog Carlo .. ..Besant the Editor	156
On Stock, the Publisher	157
Authors and Publishers	157
Fur Prædestinatus..	157
A Deodand	157
"Jedburgh Justice"	158
Life and Death	158
The Vegetarian Speaks	158
Darwin v. Moses	159
"Proprium est Odisse quem Læseris"	159
"Sirs, Ye are Brethren"	159
"Divide et impera"	160
On an Ill-appointed Marriage	160
Eve and the Serpent	160
On Lord Sackville closing Knowle Park	160
On a recent Election at Guildhall	161
Thorley's Cattle Food	161
Servants' Excuses ..	161
On a Lady sending Lilies to Church	161
Restitution of Conjugal Rights	162
Collisions	162
On a Certain Publisher	162
A Good Investment	163
A Thought on Death	163

PART III.—LAYS OF VENTNOR.

Preliminary Lines ..	164
Lonely? In Praise of Ventnor	164
A Soft Answer	166
"Good Lord, Deliver me"	168
The Battle of the Flowers, I. and II.	168, 169
The Donkeys' Complaint..	170
The Triumph of the Donkeys	171
The Old Elm Tree at St. Catharine's	172
Three Rival Bands	172
Shanklin v. Ventnor	173
"The Twa Dogs"	173
Another Version of the Same	174
Eider and Eider-down	175
My Latest Dream	175
On the Death of Mrs. Judd	176
On the Portrait of Dr. A. H. Hassall	176

PART I.

SERIOUS AND SENTIMENTAL.

PATIENT GRISELDA.*

"Ye who believe in affection that hopes and endures, and is patient,
Ye who believe in the beauty and strength of a woman's devotion,
List to the mournful tradition."—LONGFELLOW.

---

*The Story of Griselda, which forms the concluding Novel of the Tenth day in the Decameron of Boccaccio, is the most touching of all the tales which make up that most witty and amusing book; and these lines are only an attempt to put the story simply and plainly into blank verse. The Story is placed in the mouth of the Clerk of Oxenford in the Canterbury Tales of Chaucer, who says that he learned it from Petrarch. Some twenty different versions of the story in French were known to exist as early as the 15th century; it has also been translated into Latin; it has been made the subject of more than one play in French and in English. The subject has also been dramatized by my friend, Sir Edwin Arnold. Ellis, in his notes to Way's Fabliaux, tells us that in Griselda its author "intended to describe a perfect female character, exposed to the severest trials, submitting without a murmur to unmerited cruelty, disarming her tormentor by gentleness and patience, and finally recompensed for her virtues by transports rendered more exquisite by her sufferings."

I.

'Mong the gay nobles of Firenze's plains,
Though still a ruddy stripling with fair cheek
And raven locks, not one in prowess vied
With Gualtiero, by ten male descents
Count of Saluzzo. For he sat his steed
As none beside; and when he blew the horn

B

And sallied to the field with hawk and hound,
All people cried, "Behold the noble son
"Of noble sires, the glory of his race."
Proud was Saluzzo of her youthful count:
For sooth he was of a right ancient line
The only hope; and fear was in the hearts
Of Gualtiero's vassals, day and night,
That should some accident by flood or field
Betide their lord, that fair domain might pass
To distant strangers—men both rude and fierce.

Now thrice six years had passed since first he
A tiny infant at his mother's knee   [played
In fair Saluzzo's halls; but she, worn down
With saddest heritage of widowed woe,
All broken-hearted when scarce past her prime,
To her last rest had gone. Gualtiero mused
Upon her memory, oft would dwell upon
The soft, dark lineaments of her sweet face.
Such thoughts would temper and subdue to tears
The pride which smouldered in his breast; for she
Had ruled his wayward temper as a child,
And as he grew to boyhood. He recalled
The long dark tresses of her raven hair
Which she would bind across her marble brow,
Her tender, loving eyes, her princely mien,
And the white flowing veil which swept athwart
The sable tokens of her widowed state.

And he would cry, when weary of the chase,
"O! the drear sadness of this lonely state,
"The vacant chamber where my mother spun,
"The vacant chair wherein my mother sate,
"She whom they say my father 'Constance' called!
"When shall these halls such other inmate greet
"As shall be fit to stand where Constance stood?

"No, that can never be: I'll hie me then
"Back to the chase, and in my hounds and hawks
"Find some poor solace for a mother's loss.
"I see no maidens, and I care to see
"None, who resemble her in beauty, or
"In priceless, peerless worth: and yet 'tis hard
"To live unloved, to see no loving face,
"To feel no loving hand, to know no heart
"That beats and throbs responsive to one's own.
"My mother's peer is far to seek; and I
"Will ne'er disgrace her memory, nor will take
"A partner to myself unworthy her."

Meantime a murmur in Saluzzo's streets
Is buzzed, then noised abroad; then rumour wakes
Her hundred tongues; and wrathful citizens
Cry out in discontent.
    "It shames us much
"Year after year to see untenanted
"Those halls in which the noble Constance shone
"Our gracious Countess, cheered each burgher's heart
"By kindly word or deed of charity.
"See how unpeopled now our market-place,
"Our streets our shops, once busy haunts of men,
"And hives of industry; how stand our looms
"All idle, and how idleness breeds sloth,
"And sloth breeds poverty and miscontent.
"Oh that our Count would choose some noble bride
"Of Venice, Padua, or of Modena,
"And give us back a Constance in his choice."

It happened thus one day, one festival:
High mass was over, and, as wont it was,
The burghers of Saluzzo and their wives,
Children and all, a goodly retinue,

Walked on the terrace 'neath the castle wall
To greet the Count upon his natal day.
And Gualtiero stood amid the crowd
Conspicuous by gay dress and manly gait,
And easy courteous bearing; and he spake
Kind words of friendship now to this, now that,
Waving his pluméd bonnet to the crowd.

   Stepped forth six burghers from the rest, and said,
" Most noble Count, son of a noble sire,
" Nor a less noble mother's son, we crave
" Audience and due attention at thine hands.
" We were thy father's vassals; we are thine;
" And that allegiance that we paid to him
" We owe his son; nor shall it e'er be said
" That we were wanting in due loyalty.
" We love thy mother's and thy father's child,
" And we would shed for thee, if need, our blood.
" Thou wilt not therefore turn a cold, deaf ear
" To our entreaty if plain words we speak.

   " Our city prospers, as thou seest amiss:
" Its trade, its commerce, and its populace
" Are not as once they were, and still might be;
" And much it troubles us lest aught befal
" Our youthful Count, and this free, loyal state
" Pass to the appanage of unworthy lords.
" There is no heir to thine ancestral line;
" And, reft of her who queenlike should preside
" Over thy court, whose presence should be felt
" Like that of the meridian sun, to shed
" Light, warmth and plenty round, our city pines.
" 'Tis but a little step from murmurings deep
" To discontent, and wrath rebellion breeds.
" Leave us not then without a lord, nor live
" Heirless, but think thee of our earnest prayer.

"And if thou lov'st the chase and still wilt seek
"The wild boar's lair, a huntsman, nor wilt heed
"Thoughts of young love, to us entrust the task
"To find a mate well worthy of thy bed."

"Right worthy friends and neighbours," he replied,
"That which ye bid me do I had resolved
"Wary to shun; for though full many a maid
"Of Northern Lombardy or our Tuscan towns
"Would gladly call her Gualtiero's bride,
"Saluzzo's Countess, yet my love to her
"Who gave me birth, whom still ye burghers love,
"Forbids me to ambition aught that is
"Inferior to herself; and many a mile
"Well might I traverse both by land and sea,
"Ere I beheld her equal, or in mien,
"Or in a loving, loyal, trusting heart.
"Peerless she was, and peerless yet she stands,
"Nor can ye point to her that is her peer.
"Yet it mislikes me that this city fair
"Should risk its being or its weal on one
"Who bears and carries no enchanted life.
"So masters, an it please ye, I will strive
"Against mine inclination, and will seek
"A maiden who shall be unto your hearts:
"And if beside she be to me, good sirs,
"A loyal friend, submissive, fond, and true,
"It may be that I even shall rejoice
"To give a Countess to this city fair.
"But stay, one warning. Whom I choose as bride
"Of Gualtiero, be she who she may,
"Of royal, noble, or ignoble blood,
"Ye swear to me, right worthy sirs, that ye
"And all my people loyally accept
"And reverence, as though she were a queen

"Of gay Ravenna, or of Milan proud,
"Aye, or of fair Firenze, come what may."

 He spoke: the burghers swore, and straight retired;
The gay crowd parted, and the terrace-path
Lay lonely and deserted, as in knots
Of twain and three the burghers homeward paced,
Much pondering in perplexèd wonderment.
And Gualtiero called his hound, and stroked
His courser's arched neck, then as half inclined
To wish his words unsaid, stood in amaze;
Like erst Adonis, when he heard the voice
Of Aphroditè by his hunter's side,
And heedless spurned and scorned her proffered love.

II.

 On the grey slope of an Abruzzian hill,
Where a steep bridle-path leads down the road
To a grim convent's portal, and a cross
Marks limit to the consecrated ground,
Fringed with a scanty flower-bed and o'erhung
By a dark grove of olives, intermixed
With pale ceringos and acacia bowers,
A humble cottage stood. Giannuculo,
Its tenant, was a labourer of the soil,
And sixty summer suns had bronzed his cheek.
With him there dwelt a daughter, passing fair,
The envy of each youthful villager
On this side and on that. Her girlhood now
Was scarcely passing into womanhood;
And yet she showed a woman's care of him
Who was her sire, and who with duteous lips
Said daily "*De profundis*" for the soul
Of her departed mother. She was fair;

But not so fair as modest, pure, and chaste.
A violet from beneath a moss-clad stone*
Peeping in early spring-tide scarce did caste
Its glance more shyly forth upon the vale
Than did Griselda when she spoke and smiled.
And prized was she much by her rustic sire,
Who called her his fair flow'ret ; and his friend,
The *padre* of the hamlet, vowed with pride
That ne'er was beauty more allied with worth.
" Thrice happy," would he say, " the swain who'er
" Shall win her heart's affection, and shall call
" Griselda mistress of his humble home."

It chanced one day, one summer eventide,
A stranger gay, with horses, hawks, and hounds,
Weary with sport, rode homeward to the town,
And down the western slope of the tall hill
Nearing the convent portal, reined his steed,
Then lighting, walked along and held his rein.
Passing the cottage of Giannuculo
The stranger stayed a moment, and addressed
A word of greeting to the old man's ear,
As basking in the evening sun he sat.
" How now ? what, all alone ? and hast thou none,
" Or wife, or child, to cheer thy loneliness ?
" 'Faith by our Lady, you and I, good sir,
" Are our own masters."
      Scarce the word was spoke,
When, singing as she tripped along the path,
From the pure fountain at the garden side,
Bearing a draught of water fresh and clear,
Griselda came. The stranger stepped aside,
Much wondering to behold vision so fair.

---

   *A violet by a mossy stone,
   Half hidden from the eye.
        WORDSWORTH.

Then spoke his heart unto his inner self,—
" Poor though she be, that maiden fair, I vow,
" Before this moon hath waned and waxed again—
" No ! that were long to wait; this very eve—
" Shall be Saluzzo's countess and the bride
" Of Gualtiero !"
                And no sooner thought
Had passéd into speech, than he declared
Unto Giannuculo his love.
                        " I read
" In this sweet maiden's features all I seek
" To gladden and to grace the palace halls
" In which erewhile my mother Constance shone.
" I am Saluzzo's count ; and in her eyes
" I see the eyes of Constance ; in her gait,
" The princely queen-like mien ; those raven locks,
" The marble of her forehead,—all, I swear,
" Remember me of what my mother was."

 " You do much honour to our poor estate,
" Most noble Count ; and if it be thy will
" To wed my daughter, let that will be done.
" Only I fear that she may climb too high,
" And take her seat upon a throne awhence
" One day her downfall shall more grievous be."

 "Fear not, my friend ; but first, in order due,
" 'Tis fitting that I question her one word.
" I am Saluzzo's Count ; I seek thy hand,
" Thy hand and heart ; say, wilt thou bend thy will,
" Whole and entire, and in no stinted share,
" Unto my will obedient, *come what may ;*
" Nor shrink to render service to thy lord,
" Who loves thee, but whose will must be thy law ?"

    The maiden laid her pitcher on the ground ;
Stood for a moment half amazed and shy,

Then looked to heaven, as though she would attest
The saints to her resolve, and said "I will."

    He led her by the hand, and bade her strip
Her poor apparel, save one threadbare smock;
Then called for richest garments, silken hose,
Tunic and corselet, and a flowing robe
Of satin tissue; and a coronet
Placed on her unkempt hair, and cried aloud,
As flocked the wond'ring rustics to the view,
" Behold the maiden whom I make this day
" My wife, Saluzzo's Countess." Greeting next
Honest Giannuculo, forthwith he set
Griselda on a palfrey, and she rode
On his left hand straight to the palace gates.
Forth came the heralds at the gladsome news,
And cried, " Behold our lord Gualtiero's self,
" And greet his bride with loud and glad acclaim,
" For she is worthy of a princely mate."
Loud trumpets echoed back the voice of praise,
Pealed the sweet bells of churches, blazed the fires,
And glad Saluzzo woke to life once more.

III.

Twelve months, twelve happy months have come
       and gone,
And Gualtiero with a deep'ning love
Doth cherish his fair bride, and ever fresh
Appear the tokens of his fond regard.
But when to a wife's title she did add
The name of mother, and a daughter fair
She bore, his countenance became enstranged:
Harsh words he uttered in his angry mood;—
" What; can ye bear no son? In vain have I
" Sought out a bride in thee, if issue none

" Or none but female issue be my lot.
" Hark how my subjects mutter in their scorn,
" Curse thy mean parentage and poor estate:
" Thou art not what I hoped to find in thee.
" That child thou nursest in thine arms, I cast
" Upon the bleak hill's side, to dogs and birds
" A fitting prey. Now dost thou know thy fate!"
  To whom Griselda, " Good, my lord; but why
" Thus tax me with reproof? Nay, deal with me
" As best befits thy weal and happiness.
" Did I not promise fealty to my lord?
" I bow my will submissive unto thine.
" I am by birth the meanest of the race
" That owns thee master; and I was not fit
" To sit advanced to such high dignity.
" Nay, send me back unto that humble cot
" Whence thou didst lead me, a plain village maid,
" Robeless and crownless, rich in nought beside
" But in the love of him who sought my love,
" And in the gift of honest maidenhood.
" Nay, if thou wilt be hard of heart, then take
" My tender infant, cast her to the wolves
" That prowl around th' Abruzzi; she is thine:
" Say, wer't thou not thyself her father true?
" Yet cast her not unto the wolves, with tears
" I do implore thee,—with a mother's tears—
" *Unless it be thy will;* and if so be,
" *Thy will and God's be done.*"
      Stepped forth at this
Two men, fierce scowling, and with threatening
    glance
Drew daggers from their sides, nor spake a word.
Yet stood Griselda still, and kissed her babe,
And made the holy sign upon her brow,
And bound a tiny cross around her neck,

And only cried, "*Thy will and God's be done!*
" It may be that the holy saints who guard
" Our marriage bed, will to my prayer give ear,
" And grant me yet a son in face and form
" To image forth his father's lineaments;
" That son shall be a bond between us yet,
" And recompense my loss. *Thy will be done.*"

Twelve months, twelve anxious months have rollèd on,
And to the vacant cradle of the babe
Succeeds a son. Fair was his cheek, and bright
His eye, and dark his hair, like Constance's.
He grew to prattle on Griselda's knee,
To know her voice, and call her 'mother dear,'
Nor shrank in terror at the plumèd crest
Of Gualtiero.

    As she sat one day
Upon the terrace, playing with her boy,
The father stern approached, and threatening, spake;
"Griselda, thou art pure, and good, and true,
" Nor ever hast thou failed in loyalty
" To me thy lord. My will is thine. 'Tis well
" It should be so. Then hear. My burghers all
" Mutter in silence or aloud complain,
" A humble peasant's child should be my heir,
" Their future lord. 'Tis therefore meet that thou
" Give up this boy to share his sister's fate,
" And then return to that was once thy home
" Hard by the Convent gate; Giannuculo
" Will give thee welcome, and his aged heart
" Haply thou yet mayst cheer. Meantime my soul
" Yearns for a nobler mate. Say what thou wilt,
" My mind is fixed; and ere to-morrow's sun
" Hath set, thy father's door receives thee back
" As naked as thou camest thence to me.
" And for thy son—"

" Nay, good my lord, I bow
" Unto thy voice, thy word, thy will—my law,
" I bow, obedient; though it wrings my heart,
" My very heart of hearts, not to lay down
" The coronet thou didst place upon my brow,
" But the dear name of mother, and to see
" Thy henchman bear the sweet fruit of my womb
" To perish on the hills. Nay, cast him not
" Unto the wolves, as erst——But nay, my tongue
" Shall ne'er give utterance to reproachful word.
" Gualtiero's wife shall ever worthy be
" Of her who was his mother. But my son—
" Cast him not to the wolves, *unless it be*
" *Thy will: and then thy will and God's be done.*
" Yet ere I go upon my lonely road,
" A wife discrowned, yet scarce dishonourèd,
" One word I crave. This crown, these jewels bright,
" This silk attire, yea, and this golden ring
" With which thou didst espouse my maiden hand,
" I give thee back, for they are thine,—no gifts,
" But only lent me for a little space.
" You bid me take the dowry that I brought;
" You need no teller for to count the dross,
" Nor I a purse to wrap it in, far less
" A sumpter-horse or mule to carry it.
" Naked you took me from my father's hands,
" And naked I return, such as I came,
" Bereft of nought, save only maidenhood;
" That jewel thou canst ne'er give back to me.
" One little boon I ask: to hide my shame
" Grant me one body-robe in lieu of that
" Which thou, my lord, didst take. *Thy will be done.*"

  * * * * * *

Clad in one modest smock of simple white,

Ere that the morrow's sun had set, rode forth
In tears, Griselda, to her father's gate,
Weeping herself, yet more her infant son—
One faithful servant her sole retinue,
And bath'd in tears, he led her palfrey back.
Then quick she donned again her beggar dress,
And fetched the pitcher from the well, and swept
Her father's floor, and cheered his aching heart,
Forgetful of her woe; or, if she thought,
'Twas for her children.—Were they dead and gone,
Torn by fierce wolves, or men as fierce as they?
Or did they live? And she would cross her breast,
And cry, "Oh! holy Mother of the Christ,
" Grant me the gift of patience, to control
" The throbbings of a wife's, a mother's heart.
" God's will and thine be done, and his to whom
" I still am true, a wife and yet no wife."

Ten years, ten weary years have rollèd on;
Griselda sits within her father's cot,
And save unto the village chapel, or
The convent gate, ne'er hath she wandered forth,
But ever-patient and without complaint,
Bearing the silent burden of her woe,
Hath lived an angel's life. Giannuculo
Blessed day by day his child, so pure, so fair,
So woe-worn, yet so meek amid her woes;
And cried " Heaven pardon him who did thee
    wrong!"

One summer morn, twelve years the very day
Since that Griselda in her cottage home
Had first beheld her lord—in hottest haste
A horseman reins his steed before the door
Where sits Giannnculo in pensive mood.
" The count, my lord and master and thine own,

" Hath sent to call thy daughter, fair Griselde,
" Upon the pain of fealty, to appear
" This day within his palace gates. Once more
" Saluzzo joys to learn its lord, the Count,
" Our gracious Gualtiero, hath prepared
" His halls to welcome a new bride, as fair
" As was Griselda, and of nobler blood.
" To-morrow,—for the Court of Rome meanwhile
" Hath granted dispensation for the deed—
" God's priest before God's altar forth shall stand
" And publicly proclaim our noble chief
" And a fair daughter of Count Panago,
" In God's name and the Church's, man and wife.
" And need there is that every chamber shine
" Beswept and garnished, that the palace smile
" Resplendent, as befits a bridal day.
" Griselda's hands are not ill-used to toil;
" Griselda's eyes will keep good watch and ward
" Over the kitchen and the banquet hall.
" Say, shall she come obedient to my voice?"

    The morrow's sun arose. Griselda went,
She swept the palace halls, garnished the floor,
The couches, each familiar guest-chamber
Dressed in its gayest colours, and came forth
To greet the Countess as she stepped from off
Her palfrey at the gate.

                      The guests are there,
And all is expectation, and the feast
Will soon begin.
                " And now, what thinkest thou,
" Griselda, of my bride?" the Count exclaimed.
" Sooth she is fair, yes, passing fair, and fit
" To deck these halls, as none afore her was.
" And, if she be as good as she is fair,

" You may reign happy in Saluzzo's halls,
" And hand your heritage to a long line
" Of noble sons, sprung from your princely loins.
" But oh! if I may breathe one prayer, I pray
" Thou mayst not rack this youthful maiden's heart
" As thou has racked another's.   Yet withal
" *Thy will, my lord, and God's own will be done.*
" Young is thy bride, and nurtured tenderly;
" I was a tougher sapling, yet I knew
" To bend me to the storm, as one who learnt
" Life's fitful moods, and as a child was schooled
" To hardships, aye, from earliest infancy.
" Yet stay—What means this locket, and this cross?
" It is the same which twelve long years ago
" I bound about that neck—the neck of her,
" My first-born child! Oh! God, and saints of
            Heaven,
" Do I yet see mine own, my long-lost child?
" And by her side, so like their father's face,
" Her brother? or doth sight bemock my heart,
" My mother's heart, and is it all a dream?
" *God's will and Gualtiero's will be done!*"
She spoke, and swooning, sank upon the ground.

  Then rose the Count, and every lip was still,
Hushed in amazing silence: and he spoke:
" Ye burghers of Saluzzo, trusty friends,
" Worshipful sirs, ye see before ye here
" Griselda, my most spotless, noblest bride.
" This lady who hath stepped from off her steed,
" And sitteth in the seat of honour there,
" Is not a child of noble Panago,
" But sprung from me, her sire.   Griselda, see
" In her thy long lost daughter, and in him,
" This noble youth, thy well-belovéd son.
" O, fair thou art, Griselda, passing fair;

" Yet not so fair as noble. Say, was ere
" Daughter of Eve, who could so far forget
" Herself, her children, all save loyalty
" To her espousèd lord? who patient thus
" Could brook to see her children wrenched perforce
" And cast unto the wolves, nor yet complain,
" Nor utter word of tenderest reproach?
" Nay, that which saints and angels could not do,
" Griselda, thou hast done; therefore to me
" Dearer thou art than all the world beside;
" And once more I do greet there here before
" Th' assembled burghers of this city fair,
" The partner of my crown, my bed, my life.
" And here, in token of my words, I vow
" This day unto the very end of time
" Hallowed shall be through all my wide domains;
" And thou, Griselda, saint and wife in one,
" Shall stand in marble in our city's streets,
" Patient Griselda, fair, and good, and great.
" Much have I wronged thee; but 'tis thine to cast
" A tender eye, forgiving all that wrong.
" It is for man to err; but to forgive
" Belongs to woman and high heaven alone."

*   *   *   *

And is Griselda but a thrice told tale?
And can we read no lesson in her life?
Yes, such a thing there lives as biding faith,
Undoubting and unswerving loyalty,
In wedded love, yes, and in friendship too.
Be it a man's, be it a woman's heart,
Let time go on, let months roll on to years,
And years to ages, yet he conquers who
Ever endures and patiently abides,
Till heaven doth righteously " defend the right."

In every sufferer in the sacred cause
Of loyalty and love Griselda lives;
For pure affection " seeketh not her own,
" Is not provoked by trifles, **evil** none
" Doth think, **but** bideth patiently, all things
" Suffereth, **endureth, beareth,**" to the end.

Yes, years may come, **and** years may glide away,
Fashions and **forms** may change, and **raven** locks
Turn grey with care, and hearts grow dull and cold
That once would beat responsive to our own;
But loyal friendship, friendly loyalty,
Holds on its **even** course, steers to the **port**
Of **peace** and **rest,** though storms may rage without.
Then fret not, loyal and devoted soul.
The fiery torment that long time did wrack
Griselda's heart may wrack thine own; **and yet**
There is a silvery lining **to** each cloud,
And who " in patience doth his soul possess "
Or soon or late **he** shall the victor be.*

---

*If we may believe what Walter Savage Landor says in his Pentameron, Petrarch wrote thus only a few days before his death: " The touching story of Griseldis has been laid up in my memory, " that I may relate it in my conversations with my friends. A " friend of mine at Padua, a man of wit and knowledge, " undertook to read it aloud; but he had scarcely got through " half of it, when his tears prevented his going on. He attempted " it a second time, but his sobs and sighs obliged him to desist. " **Another of my** friends determined on the same experiment, and " having read **it** from beginning to end without the least alteration " of voice, said, on returning the book, " It must be **owned that** " this **is** an affecting story; and **I could** have **wept over it if I** " could have believed it true, **but there** never was **and never will** " be a woman like Griseldis."

GHISMONDE THE FAIR.*

OMNIA VINCIT AMOR. VIRGIL, ECL. X. 69.

*This story is taken from Boccacio's Decameron; it has been versified by Dryden, and it formed the subject of a drama by Robert Wilmot, which was acted before Queen Elizabeth at the Inner Temple, in 1568, (see Dodsley's collection of Old Plays, vol. ii.) The substance of the story has been made familiar by a painting attributed to Corregio, in which Sigismunda is represented as weeping over the heart of her lover; and the same subject was treated, though in a very different style, by Hogarth. The story has also been rendered into Latin prose by L. Aretine, into Latin Elegiac verse by Filippo Beroald, and also into Italian. It forms the subject of no less than five Italian tragedies, one of which, " La Ghismonda," was at one time attributed, though falsely, to Torquato Tasso. Some liberties have been taken with the story in the present version.

In fair Salerno, hard by Napoli,
As wise in counsel as in prowess bold,
Yet proud withal, but not so proud as brave,
His grey hair whitening with the snows of years,
Tancredo reigned as prince. His city shone
In arts conspicuous far above her peers,
In physic, law, and sage theology.
But court nor life of state did Tancred keep;
For, ere he reached the noontide of his life,
Fate had borne off the idol of his heart,
His partner in twelve years of wedded love,
And left him ruler o'er a widow'd hall.
But in her place there grew to womanhood
A daughter fair of form, Ghismonda named;
And she would cheer the old man's heart and sing
The songs he loved to hear of war and chase;
And she would play the cithern or the lute;
And she would oft caress his hawk and hound
And courser gay; and as she walked along
The people cried, " Behold the daughter fair
Of a fair mother, and as good as fair."

And years rolled on ; and she had won the heart,
The heart and hand of Capua's princely son :
But ere twelve months had waxed and waned again,
Her Lord lay stretch'd upon the battle-field,
And she had donned the weeds of widowhood ;
Then back returned unto her father's halls,
Though young in years yet childless.
                              So she mourn'd
In secret silence ; and she pined, and grew
Weary of life and life's sad desolateness.

Meantime Tancredo, shrinking from the gaze
Of his own people, lived an inner life,
Thoughtful, retired, much pondering on the past,
Yet more upon the future. He would spend
Long days in silence, and would muse alone
Upon his Castle terrace ; and he grew
Moody and speechless; for no friend drew near
To break Salerno's dull monotony.
But Ghismonde, she was young, and of young love
And love's delights had tasted ; and she pined
In weariness, unmated.
                       Now it chanced
One day she crossed the market-place afoot,
From mass returning or from vesper prayer ;
Dropped down from her fair neck a tiny cross,
And string of beads from off her rosary.

Haply Guiscardo, though he was the son
Of poor but honest parents, and his cheeks
And arms with daily labour were abronzed,
Stepp'd forth and picked the golden treasure up,
And handed it to Ghismonde with a bow,
So graceful and so gentle that he smote
Her inmost heart, and stole her soul away.
Guiscardo she with kindly words dismissed,

And begged that he would come the morrow's noon
Unto the palace to receive a gift.
" No gift, my gracious lady, I desire ;
Your thanks are my reward."
                      He came and sang
A rural song such as the goatherds sing
By flowry Pæstum and on Silare's banks.
Ghismonde admired his rustic muse, but more
His bearing, noble, yet all rustic too ;
And most his stately figure, and his limbs
Lithe, supple, well-proportioned ; and she thought
Seldom was seen on noble face a smile
More comely and more truthful.
                          So to tell
The story briefly, 'twas the old, old tale
That Eve to Adam told in Paradise,
And that our parents each to other tell
From that day to the present. Flesh and blood
Was Ghismonde and no angel ; and she burnt
With no angelic fires. Her pulse throbbed quick,
Her eye it glistened, and her fair cheek flushed.
Guiscardo saw ; and as no laggard pressed
The soft advantage, nor was Ghismonde coy.
And though no marriage knot the priest did tie,
Yet love found out a stealthy secret way
To vindicate his own.
                        Shaded by shrubs
Beside the Castle ran a terrace walk,
Above a bower with tangled weeds o'ergrown
And idle briars in rich profusion mix'd.
Here haply Tancred in his youth had oft
Sat late and early at the drinking bout ;
And far in th' inmost corner of the bower,
A door brought 'neath the terrace to the steps
And winding stair that to the chamber led

Where Ghismonde tenanted her couch. They say
"**Love** laughs **at** locksmiths, or he finds the key."
So rarely at the midnight **hour** the moon
Peer'd into Ghismonde's casement and beheld
One only tenant of that chamber-room.
And they were happy, those devoted ones,
And reck'd not of the hours that flew betimes
Too fast for lovers in their madden'd mood.

It chanced **one** summer morn, ere **yet** the sun
Rose high **in** heaven, Tancredo early paced
His battlements, and adown the terrace walked ;
When issuing **forth** from Ghismond's chamber came
Radiant with **joy** and smiling as the day
Guiscardo's **self**.

"**How** now, and whence art thou?
And whence thus early com'st thou here? Speak
out.
Methinks that secret chamber is fit place
For thieves **or robbers ; and** thou dost not seem
Some weary, way-**worn, foot-sore** traveller.
Hah **!** and the plume thou wearest scarce **is** fit
For **such as thee**—for walkers **of** the night.
Nay, but it is Ghismonda's craft. I saw
Her **fair hands** work it, **when** but yester eve
She **sat beside me.** Surely ne'er did she
Bedeck thee thus. Speak, caitiff, or I swear
By heaven, **this** sword shall **smite thee to** the
ground."

"**Hold**, sir, thy sword. Thy daughter Ghismonde
fair,
Gave me yestreen this plume ; I prize it much,
For 'tis to me a sign of somewhat more.
I have her love, her very heart of hearts.
Faith, love is stronger, sir, than you or I."

"Out on thee, caitiff vile; what? shall I see
My house dishonoured and my princely name
In foul disgrace o'erwhelmed, and tame stand by,
Nor smite to earth the doer of the wrong!"
"No wrong, good sir; your daughter sooth is fair,
And young and gracious; but she holds herself
Her own, not thine; she was of age to wed
Five summers since; she to herself belongs:
And if she love Guiscardo, this at least
Guiscardo boasts, he never sought her love,
Which proffered came, unbidden and unbought."

"'Tis well, thou diest not now; nor shall this sword
Reek with thy blood. Yet get thee from my sight;
For if again within these walls I see
Thy form unwelcome, then with many a prayer
Vainly thou'lt wish never thy foot had strayed
Within the precincts of my castle gates.
Begone, or quick prepare to meet thy doom."

* * * * *

Now weeks rolled on, and rumour nois'd abroad
Brought to Tancredo's ear unwelcome news,
That Ghismonde, though no wife, would soon become
A mother, and bring foul disgrace upon
The princely line whose scutcheon and fair shield
Had ever spotless been imaginèd.
Then rose the wrath within him, and he spake:

"The man that hath this evil wrought shall die;
Tancredo's shield shall never know a stain:
Or, if a blot befal it, he that cast
That blot shall wipe it with his own heart's blood.
By this my sword Guiscardo, as I swore,
Shall ne'er die stricken; but he dies forthwith,
Nor lives to see the son Ghismonda bears

Within her womb. Open the prison gate
And cast Guiscardo into dungeons deep;
For e'er the third day's morn arise, he dies:
My trusty henchman's hands shall teach him thus
Folly to work amain. My word is law.

  "Mercy, my father, be thou merciful.
Nay rather be thou just, not merciful,"
Ghismonda cried: "he is no caitiff base,
Guiscardo; but my hope, my stay, my love.
I am but flesh and blood, and I am young;
I did but yield myself to love's own law;
And he is worthy of my love. 'Tis true
Noble he is not by Salerno's rule,
And heralds count him not of noble blood;
But he doth cherish a right noble heart,
Such heart as well deserves enoblement;
And if he be both honest and unblest
With this world's wealth, father, the blame is thine.
He shall not die; my fate and his are one.
Or if, Guiscardo, death await thee, then
The same death on that self-same day awaits
Me too, thy daughter, and my unborn child.
Nay, father! hear me, father! spare thy tears;
Spare them, lest haply thou have need of tears
E'er many a sun hath risen: for thou wilt weep
Bereft of me thy child, thy daughter dear."

  Came the third day: bearing a golden urn,
And in that urn a mangled bleeding heart,
Drew near a servant.
           Ghismonde sat, nor spake
Or word of grief or overflow of love;
But firm in her resolve she calmly said;
"Wisely, Tancredo, in a golden cup
Thou didst enshrine this heart, for nought save gold

Were fit material to receive the gift.
I thank thee, father, for thy latest boon."

She said, and took a poison'd goblet down
From off the shelf, and quaff'd Tancredo's health;
And with her tears thrice and again she laved
The lov'd remembrance of Guiscardo's self.
"And thou art dead! Yes, yet a little space,
And I too follow thee, dear heart of hearts.
Only one boon I crave at Tancred's hands.
As join'd in life so too conjoined in death
Let us twain lie beneath the grassy sod;
And on our tomb be written but the words,
"Guiscardo and Ghismonda lie below;
Stranger, they 'lov'd not wisely, but too well.'"

* * * * *

And Tancred mourn'd the deed that he had done,
And fain would have recalled the word of doom
Which reft him of a daughter; and he rais'd
Above the grave which held their bodies twain
A noble monument to tell the tale:
And they who to Salerno's shrine may come
To distant ages shall the story hear
How Ghismonde and Guiscardo lov'd and died.

THE CAPUCHIN CONVENT.*

NEMO SERIO PŒNITENS AD DEUM SERO VENIT.

*The substance of this story is taken from a sermon preached by Philip de Narni, a monk of the Capuchin order, in the Cathedral of Vienna, during the Pontificate of Gregory XV. (A.D. 1621—1623). Some portion of the sermon will be found in "Mediæval Preachers and Mediæval Preaching," by the late Rev. J. M. Neale, D.D., Warden of Sackville College, East Grinstead.

Far from the haunts of men, beside a gorge

Where Danube rolls his waters deep and strong,
In a sequestered vale, 'mid darkening groves
Of pine and chestnut and pale sycamore,
A convent stood. Tall were its portal gates,
And from the niche above, with downcast eye,
Bearing the Holy Babe of Bethlehem,
The maiden mother stood and smiled in stone.*
The western hills sloped with fair vineyards crowned;
And rich and luscious was the wine that flowed
From out the Convent's press. Its garners teem'd
With every manner of store; and in its meads
Beneath the Convent walls fat beeves reclined,
Or pastured on the hill-side. Clear and deep,
Hard by, the lake wherein the lazy carp
Would oft in summer sunshine bask, as though
They too had drank the air of indolence;
And passing fair the river, that did cleave
This mead from that: in it the largest trout
Sported at will, or gave a dainty dish
To the proud Abbot and his daintier Monks.

The envy of all neighbours, high and low,
Noble and gentle, or of lowlier blood,
The reverend Fathers all of the Orders Grey,
Meantime, oblivious of the rigid rule
Of him, their founder, Francis of Assise,
Eat, drank, and slept, or merrily beguiled
The vacant hours; and, so that Mass were said,

---

†St. Francis of Assissi, the founder of the Franciscans and Capuchins, had a singular devotion to the Mother of God, whom he chose for the special Patroness of his order. . . . He was not able to satiate the tender affection of his heart by repeating often with incredible sweetness the Holy name of Jesus under the appellation of the " Little Babe of Bethlehem."—*Butler's Lives of the Saints*, Oct. 4.

Prime, Nones, Tierce, Vespers, Compline, were
    forgot.
Nay, and they never kept a Lenten fast ;
Nor did chill hunger's wholesome discipline
Remind them holiest vows were on them still ;
Those vows that Francis taught his sons to take,
To clothe the naked, feed the famishing,
Abjure the world, and mortify the flesh.
More tuns of wine lay mellowing in their bins
Than could supply a thousand altar's use ;
Aye,—so the neighbours said in bitterest jibe—
Well nigh enough to turn the convent mill ;
And though they wore their founder's habit yet,[*]
Grey cowl and cloak, and girded them with cords,
And barefoot walked, yet still the brethren proved
"The cowl it doth not always make the monk."[†]
And so from morning until night, from night
To early morning they caroused, and held
High festival, and worked their will amain.

  One solemn day, a day of penitence,
Of penitence and prayer,—for said not so
The Church's Calendar, and their own rule ?—
The brethren gathered in loose revelry
Within the walls of their Refectory room.
Loud laughter followed upon noisy song,
And noisier joke, that scarce from holy lips
Should e'er proceed, and doubtful jests, passed on

---

    [*]St. Francis contented himself with one poor coat, which he girt about him with a cord, and this was the habit which he gave to his friars. . . . It was the dress of the poor shepherds and country peasants in the parts about Assissi. The Saint added a short cloak over the shoulders, and a "capuche" to cover the head. From this the Franciscans came to be commonly called Capuchins.—*Butler's Lives of the Saints*, Oct. 4.
    [†] "*Cucullus non facit monachum.*"—*Old Proverb.*

From lip to lip, went circling all around.
High in his chair of state the Abbot sate,
And laughed and chuckled o'er the coarser mirth;
" Faith, by our Lady, ne'r was jest like that!"
Sudden, a knock sounds at the Convent gate;
The monks they start amazed, the porter quick
Hies to the door, and opens. Creaks the hinge,
The hinge, all rusty with unfrequent use:
The brother peers into the outer gloom,
And peers again. Then by the fire-light gleam
Revealed, his eye descries a thin tall man.
Is it a man, or one of mortal mould?
He wore the old grey habit, and the cowl
Familiar, and his bony feet were bare;
Ancient his shape; one grey betattered robe
Hung loose about his shoulders; and the moths
Had feasted daintily on the threadbare serge.
Athwart the bones that arched his skull and cheek,
Like rotting parchment, stretched his sallow skin;
No flesh was there, all colourless his eye,
His beard* unkempt shone with unearthly hue.
And thus in hollow and sepulchral tone
He spoke: " For God's, and His dear Mother's sake,
" Let me pass in, good sir; 'tis I who ask
" Admittance in St. Francis' name."
                                            Amazed
The porter shrank and started, (for he deemed
It was a vision from the nether world),
Fast closed the door, and faster drew the bolt,
Then sought instruction from the Abbot's chair.

   " Stands there, my lord, without the Convent gate
" A strange old man, of bony shrunken form,

---

*The Capuchins wore a black patch on the back of their habits, and their beards not shaved close, but long and clipped.

" And scarce doth seem to be of human mould,
" Save that he wears our founder's livery,
" Badge of our brotherhood ; speak thou but the
    word,
" And I admit him in St. Francis' name."

  Then rose the Abbot : " Nay, the winds howl
    fierce ;
" The snow it thickens on the dark hill-side,
" And the grey sky bespeaks a tempest-storm,
" Faith, 'tis a wintry night ; we've plenteous cheer ;
" Go, open wide the door and let him in.
" Is not our rule to practise charity ?
" So haply unawares may be this night
" We entertain an angel. What say ye,
" My reverend brethren ? Nay, then bring him in,
" And place a chair betwixt the fire and me ;
" Fill up the wine-cup high, and as he drinks,
" Bring forth a pasty and a platter, for
" Perchance he suffers hunger. Brethren all,
" Enough have we in larder and in bin,
" Aye, and in cellar too. He's thin and spare ;
" Good feasting ne'er will come amiss to him."

  The strange monk entered, bowed, and took his
    seat.
His head was shrouded with his cowl close drawn,
And not a morsel did he eat nor drink,
But silent sate, as though the world unseen
Had sent to join that awful revelry
A disembodied spirit.
                          And as he sate,
A knock was heard again. The porter gazed
Again forth into darkness, and he saw
A fearful sight. In scores and hundreds stood
There round the gates, a bony, ghastly crew

Of monks, with grisly faces; and their cowls
Waved horribly about; they stamped their feet,
As storming impotent in deadliest rage,
And their teeth chattered in the wintry wind.
  "Let them all in," aloud the Abbot cried;
"The more the merrier in these merry halls!
"We've wine enough, aye, and to spare; come, fill
"The brimming goblet, and prepare the feast:
"Our wine will last us till the crack of doom."

  And so that ghastly crew they entered in,
They clustered round the hearth, the Abbot's chair,
The pulpit steps; they thronged the vestibule;
And some sate grinning on the sounding board,
High poised in air, and shook their garments gray.
The monks they trembled, and they all turned pale,—
Pale as the new in-comers.

                    Then arose
A distant sound, as of ten thousand pines
All crackling in the flames; a deadly smell
As of flesh burning, with foul, sulphurous steam
Commingling, came upon the senses. Smote
Their knees in terror, and their coward tongues
To their mouth's roofs did cleave for very fear:
For they were face to face with monks long dead,
Their own forefathers, and whose bodies lay
Resting within the cemetery hard by,
Upon the dark hill's side beneath the Cross.

  Then up rose he who first had entered in,
The grisly stranger, and he spake: "Ye see,
"Brethren, in me one who this ancient house,
"This once revered and sacred home of faith,
"Did rule as abbot. Now the stern behest

" Of our St. Francis I obey.   I come
" To tell unwilling ears what hath befel
" Me and my brethren whom ye see with me."
" I sate within that Abbot's chair ;* I ate,
" Drank, and caroused. I worshipped not the Christ;
" I had unlearnt my ' Pater Noster ' quite ;
" I scorned to meditate on the things unseen,
" I never told my beads, I kept no fast,
" I recked not of the poor ; I feared not God
" Nor holpen man ; drove from these gates the poor,
" God's poor ; I wantoned, took my ease, and died.
" And now I am tormented in the flames—
" The gnawing flames of hell. These whom ye see,
" These were my comrades, and like me they led
" A similar life of lust and gluttony ;
" And so they suffer torment by my side.
" But in hell's lowest depths, 'mid fiercest fires,
" Such is the will of God, we still must chant
" From out unwilling lips the holy hymns,
" ' *Ave Maria,' Sancta Virginum*
" *Virgo,' and · Patri detur Gloria*
" ' *Cum Filio et ter-sancto Spiritu.*' "†

---

*St. Francis even during his lifetime found out that his spiritual children had fallen into corrupt practices. Elias of Cortona, whom he appointed Vicar General of his Order, introduced several novelties and mitigations of the monastic rule, and wore himself a habit of fine stuff, with a long hood, and fashionable sleeves. " He had," says Alban Butler, " so much regard to worldly show and advantages, that the ensigns and practices of humility and poverty became odious to him." For these and for other abuses, by which the spirit of the Order was in great danger of being extinguished, Elias was impeached and deposed by Pope Gregory IX. Again chosen General of the Order, he committed still further excesses ; was again deposed, and afterwards excommunicated. He filled the Order with great scandals and troubles, but is said to have died extremely penitent.

†The doxology, " Glory be to the Father," was a favourite aspiration of St. Francis, who would often repeat it at work and at other times.

No sooner did they hear the holy words,
The spectres rose, and shrieking, flung aloft
Their bony hands, and gnashed their grisly jaws,
Half awe-struck, half defiant ; and the roof
Rung with a loud unearthly sound, " Amen."

Then, as the noise all faintly died away,
That sad and ghastly crowd into thin air
Melted, and all was silence once again.
The rain it pelted, and the winds roared loud,
The lightning flashed and the dread thunder pealed ;
Then passed the storm, and all was peace and calm.

And once again the living monks sat round,
Aye, and the Abbot, and his face was pale.
The porter stood beside the door ; dispersed
The brethren straight, and trembling sought their
    seats.
Then rose and spake the Abbot :

                    " Brethren all,
" Give patient and attentive ear to me.
" This is a voice, not from the nether hell,
" But sent from highest heaven. Now speaks to us
" St. Francis, as he spake of old. In him
" I hear the voice of God, that bids us all
" Repent and do the former works betimes
" Worthy of penance. Be we warned in time.
" Let us then heed the prophet's awful voice.
" In sackcloth and in ashes let us all
" Do penance for our sins, and while 'tis day,
" Turn to our God." Followed a loud " Amen."

Murmur'd the monks assent, and straightway all
They change their way of life. They fast, they pray,
Scourge their proud flesh, and take the " discipline."
They sell their stores of corn, and bins of wine ;

They build anew their desolated church,
The fretted cloister, and once glorious shrine.
Straightway again its grey walls echo back
The reverend psalter and the holy hymn.
And then hard by a hospital they build,
And bid the poor man come. They feed the poor,
Nurse the plague-stricken in the hour of death,
And teach Christ's little ones the love of Heaven:
They wash the lepers' feet, and kiss their wounds,
And shrive the sinner from the stain of sin.

And years roll on to ages! ages pass;
And smiles St. Francis from his seat in Heaven,
To see the work his sons have set them to:
And so they died in sanctity and grace.

But most of all the Abbot. He had sinned—
Sinned with a grievous sin; but he betimes,
By penance and by constant fast and alms
And rigorous discipline, had put away
His sins, and washed them in his Saviour's blood.
To four-score years he lived, and saw God's peace
Rest on his brotherhood; and in green old age
Closed his calm eyes, anointed in the death
With holy oil; and, strengthened with that Bread,
The Bread of Life, breathed out his soul in peace.
God grant he may " find mercy at that day "!

THE WITCHES' SABBATH.

It is well known to the readers of curious books that the mediæval superstition of witchcraft was but a continuation of the " Phallic " worship of heathen antiquity. The "Witches' Sabbath" was the last form which the " Liberalia " of Pagan Rome assumed in Western Europe; and a few—but only a few—of its leading features are described here, for many of them will not bear description. They are mainly taken from the " *Malleus*

Maleficarum" or "*Hammer of Witches*," the work of Jacob Sprenzer and two other Germans of the fifteenth century. Reference has also been made to Bodin's treatise, *De la Démonomanie des Sorciers* (Paris 1580), and to De Lanere's *Tableau de l'Inconstancie des Mauvais Anges et Démons* (Paris, 1613), where a full account of these strange mysteries will be found. It is almost needless to remind the reader that the "Witches' Sabbath" is introduced into the scene on the Hartz Mountains, in Goethe's *Faust*.

Ye see before ye, sirs, an ancient witch,
Haggard, much worn by years, yet more by sin;
For time it hath no power upon this flesh,
Save but to wrinkle this mine outer skin,
While I drag on my being, weird and wan,
Fated for aye to live,—a death in life.
For till the day of doom I may not die.
And so I tell a tale of Vauderie;†
Whoso hath ears to hear it, let him hear.
To me time is not; what hath passed is now;
I see not things in memory, but in view,
Palpably present, e'en as but to-day.

A league from Arras, skirting dark Moflaines,
Riseth a fountain in a lonely wood,
A spot on all sides by tall pines shut in,
And dense umbrageous oaks. Hard by a dark
And sunless pool, whose stagnant depths ooze out
A foul mephitic odour. Here do we
Hold week by week our fearful revelries;
Scorn we the Christian's God, the Babe divine,
The Holy Cross, the Blessed Trinity,
And despite do unto the Sacred Name.

But in God's stead, for we have deeply drank
The philtres of apostate fiends, we take

---

†Witchcraft in the Middle Ages, was called "Vauderie" or as the word was then written, "Vaulderie." The word survives in the name of the Vaudois.

Satan our Lord, our Master, and our King;
And 'neath the form of a right noble goat,
Ancient, and snow white, with long-branching horns,
And beard down-flowing to his cloven feet,
Prostrate we all adore him; he alone
Gives forth and consecrates the wondrous oil
With which anointed we can conquer space,
Fly through thin air, and ride across the sky,
To join the fearful feast: thither we go
Born on aërial coursers, without foot,
Or hoof, or mane. Such power hath Vauderie,
And such the spells that work our will in air.

And when we reach the confines of that wood,
There is no lack of worshippers, and we
Keep awful Sabbath. Thither flock in crowds,
Burghers and nobles, prince and peasantry,
Old men and children, youths and tenderest maids,
Drawn to that grove by mystic sympathy.
Nor these alone; aye, but the tonsured there,
Shrouding their shaven heads with cloak and pall,
Stand by assistant at our fearful rites;
Apostate priests, and bishops, monks and friars.

Straight is the banquet spread; the feast begins.
With varied meats, and drinks, and luscious wines,
Our table groans, such as may best inflame
Our sensual appetite and foul lust inspire.
And he, our president, the ancient goat,
He whom ye Christians call the foul black fiend,
Nor idly call, high in a chair of state,
Of darkest ebony, sits and smiles or frowns
With awful brow upon his banqueters,
To him then bring we offerings, or of blood
Of newts or toads, or entrails of a babe
Torn from its mother's breast, or brain of ox,

Or deadliest adder's gall, or serpent's tongue,
Or wing of bat obscene, or nightly owl,
Or lock of witches' hair at midnight shorn
Beneath the pale cold crescent of the moon ;
Or, daintiest dish, the flesh of criminal,
Who high upon a gibbet in mid air
Hath hung to foulest birds and dogs a prey.

 Then, when the feast is over, and the wine,
The maddening wine, has upward sent its fumes
Into our whirling brain, we stand around,
And spit and trample on the Christian's cross,
That heavenly symbol of all-conquering love,
And curse the Saviour's name.
      Then rises straight
One of our number,—or the goat himself,
Or one of his prime followers,—and he speaks,
Words that no Christian's ear may hear.
       " Good friends,
" Nay, brethren all,—for such are we in league,
" In deadliest league combined, to war against
" The lowly Nazarite and the Christian's creed,
" Brethren in pride, in enmity, in doom :—
" 'Tis now the midnight hour, our hour to speak.
" Come forth and bold recount what valiant deed
" Of despite to the holy law of God,
" Since last we met, good friends, ye each have
   done."
Then rise we all in turn, and tell unmoved
Our witcheries, enchantments, sorceries ;
How we have lured a galleon to her doom
On the sharp rocks, or drown'd a Christian babe,
Stol'n fatted calves from out their stalls, or drained
A cow's full udder of its juicy store,

Madden'd a watch-dog, or, where cross-roads meet,
Borne off the satchel of a traveller
Footsore and weary as he lay and slept;
Or torn a corpse from 'neath the chancel stone,
Or robbed an altar of the holy pyx
And consecrated flagon, and the bread,
The holy bread, have trampled in the dust.

   Ariseth once again the ancient goat
And thanks his workers in set form of speech,
Discoursing on the mysteries of our craft,
In words of wisdom to the wise alone.*
The sermon ended, followeth loud applause.
To the sound of bells and magic music then
The tables are removed; in wildest dance
We next entwine, and lawless orgies hold,
To softest strains of wanton instruments.
Exhausted then we sink upon the ground;
The tall trees of the wood like sprites gaze on;
The fountain glistens with unearthly light:
Then a change passeth o'er the scene; the moon
Pales; rocks re-echo with the thunder-clap;
And strange weird lightnings play athwart the sky.

   Last, ere the first faint dawn of newborn day
We see appearing in the East, our King
With gracious presence breaks the banquet up,
And sends us forth on other mischiefs bent.
Our steeds again we mount, and borne on high
Through the night air we steer our homeward ways
With tortuous course o'er the tall pinewood dark,
And gain the regions waste and wide, or e'er
The cock crow forth his greeting to the sun.

        *   *   *   *   *

   *" Words eloquent to the learned," is a well-known Greek Proverb.

Such is my tale ; a tale of Vauderie :
" Whoso hath ears to hear it, let him hear."

THE MAIDENS OF VERDUN.

A Tale of 1792.

A voice of wailing and a voice of woe
In Verdun's city. For the Prussian host
Hath sat three months around her walls ; and fate
Hath wreaked fierce vengeance on her citizens.
For what no force of arms could ere effect,
Hunger hath wrought ; and in extremest strait
The city hath decreed her gates to throw
Wide open to the Prussian conqueror,
And seek for mercy in meek suppliant guise.
So better than that blood in vain be shed,
The best and noblest blood of France.
         Amain
Enter the victors ; at their head two youths,
Sons of the King, the General by their side ;
And round them gather, weary of long strife,
The citizens in hundreds, and admire
The waving plumes, the breastplates, and the swords
Of those two princely horsemen as they pass.

And now, the circuit of the city made,
Forth from her gates, all gay, past woes forgot,
Soon will there issue forth a gallant train.
Yet, stay. A whizzing sound—with treach'rous
   hand
One citizen has aimed a deadly aim,
And at the General's side falls low to earth,
Unhorsed, his heart pierced with the fatal ball,
The boldest Captain of that victor force.

"To arms! to arms! low lay in dust and blood
"The traitor city that hath dealt the blow,
"Foul deed of treachery! Go! Let loose the hounds,
"The savage hounds of war! go, fire the town!
"Our foemen to the sword! A worser fate
"Awaits the women ere the sun go down."
And there are tears and wringings of the hands,
Of women's hands, and from the children comes
A voice of wailing and a voice of woe,
Through gay Verdun.

   "Nay, but it may not be,"
Quoth a tall matron, stepping from the crowd;
"It shall not be. Send we an embassage,
"An embassage such as we women can;
"With sweetest weakness it shall plead, and bend
"The victor's heart, and save our children's blood.
"I have at home two maidens, young and fair,
"Suzanne and Gabrielle; and if none beside
"Will go upon this mission, they shall speed
"Forth to the victor's camp, unheralded,
"Alone, and conquer e'en our conquerers,
"By gentle arts—They will not plead in vain."
 And other matrons spake:—"Nay, not alone:
"Our daughters too shall go and speak the word
"That yet shall save our hearths and once-glad
   homes."

 The lots are drawn. Marguerite, and Angelique,
And Helène with the downcast tender eye;
And Jeanette, pale, her locks all flowing free;
And Claire, just budding into womanhood;
Nor one had yet a twentieth summer seen,

 And forth they walk—a goodly sight to see—
Eight maidens, two by two, and enter straight
The general's presence. In their hands they bear

Offerings of choicest fruits, of flowers that grew
By their hands tended, and a dainty store
Of comfits fit to grace a peaceful feast.

  And Gabrielle speaks:—" Good sir, our city scorns
" The foul deed done this day, and will give up
" Or banish from her gates th' assassin base.
" The citizens of gay Verdun mislike
" Foul deeds of treachery; and their tender wives
" Our mothers, forth have sent us to implore,
" On bended knees, that mercy which perchance
" One day, Sir General, thou wilt ask of heaven,
" And asking wilt receive. Then spare our blood,
" Our homes, our hearths, our lives, the little ones
" That call us sisters, nor set down the deed
" Of one unrighteous to th' account of all.
" We are but helpless maidens, as ye see;
" We love not war; for we have women's hearts;
" Timid and tender, from the name of war
" We shrink alarmed. Then list our women's prayer.
" Be just, be generous; yea, be merciful;
" Grant us our lives, and those whom yet we love
" More than our very selves, our parents dear.
" And let not fiery flames, devouring all
" Our wealth, our hearths and homes, rise up to heaven
" From Verdun's ashes."

  And the conqueror heard;
Heard, and had pity on that tender band
Of lovely maidens in their sore distress.
" Go; for your lives, your parents and your homes
" Are spared. Your weakness, maidens, is your strength;

" Ye have prevailed by woman's gentler arts
" Where nought besides could move a conqueror.
" Go ; be your mission ever thus to bless
" Those whom in time to come ye call your lords."

And so the voice of wailing and of woe
Was turned to joy in Verdun's streets that night;
And on the morrow every church pealed forth
A glad " Te Deum," as for victory.*

St. ELIZABETH OF HUNGARY.

The story of the " dear " Saint Elizabeth, as she is still called even in Protestant Germany, is full of human as well as superhuman interest. She was at one time a Queen, and at another, a beggar and an outcast; and in both states of life her sanctity shone out with equal lustre. She was the widow of the saintly King Louis of Hungary, and was only twenty-four years old when, in answer to her prayer, God called her to himself, soon after she had thrown aside her earthly crown, to enter the convent which was to be her last home on earth. See a short Life of the Saint, written by me, and published at a penny by the Catholic Truth

---

*It is sad indeed to relate that, in 1794, two years after the affair related in the above lines had taken place, these eight maidens were put on their trial before the wicked leaders of the Revolutionary party at Paris, and were found guilty of " being in league with the Prussians." Together with their mothers, and twenty-one elderly citizens of Verdun, they were sentenced to death. Shame to say, eventually six of them were executed; the lives of the two youngest were spared, the sentence in their case being commuted to imprisonment for twenty years and a day in the pillory. They were, however, released on the death of Robespierre. A little liberty has been taken with the Christian names of these maidens; but it may be interesting to know that three of them were the daughters of a M. Henri, " President du Bailliage," of Verdun, three daughters of a retired officer named Vatrin, one the daughter of the Keeper of the Woods and Forests of the Province, and one the daughter of a local magistrate. It may be added incidentally that the surrender of Verdun was one of the principal causes which brought Louis XVI. to the scaffold.

Society. There is a larger and, (as I need scarcely add) far more valuable Life of the Saint, published at Louvain in 1836, by the Comte de Montalembert.

I come, I come, my Father and my God;
Here on thine altar step to give Thee back
My royal robes, my crown, my children, all
That thou hast giv'n me; friendless now am I,
And poor of this world's goods. 'Tis better so.
What need I *now* of gold or silver, reft
Of him, my lord, my brother, and my king?
What seek I but to lay me down in peace,
Poor and contented, in the convent cell
Which henceforth shall afford a sheltering home
To these two little ones that erst I bare
To Louis, of the saintly name, my spouse?

Dead am I to the world. Its garish joys,
Its courtly splendours, can they nearer bring
Me to the joys of Heaven or Heaven to me?
Ever this seemed to me a weary world
Since happy childhood's days, when He, the Babe
Of Bethlehem, would come down in hidden guise,
And sport, my playmate, in my father's halls.*
What hath life been since then? one empty show
Of sports, of feasts, of hollowest vanities.
What earthly love? The shadow of a shade.
No. He, who turned the water-cup to wine†

---

*The Saint was regarded by her childish companions with great affection, but with even greater reverence, for they declared that the sweetness of her temper would often induce the Infant Jesus to come down and play with her.

†" Once during her husband's absence, Elizabeth sat down to her solitary meal of dry bread and water. King Louis, happening to return unexpectedly, raised his wife's cup to his lips, and to his great surprise found it full of richer wine than he had ever tasted before. Louis held his peace, but he inwardly acknowledged that the Wedding Guest of Cana had been pleased to bless the cup of cold water poured out in His name and for the love of His poor."— *Life of St. Elizabeth* by the author of *Sœur Rosalie, &c.*

For me, as erst at Cana's marriage board
He worked a miracle to set His seal
On human love, He will befriend me now,
And in His own good time will call me hence
To His true marriage-feast in Paradise.
God grant the day may soon arrive; 'tis long
To wait on earth the lingering stroke of death.
Come, friendly death, twin brother thou of sleep;
Soon shall the Spirit and the Bride say "Come."
This life must close in Death; but death in life
Eternal endeth, "where the wicked cease
From troubling, and the weary are at rest."

  O Christ, Thou know'st Thy poor have been to me
As children: I have loved them for thy sake!
O grant me then one boon. That garden fount
In which I washed their linen and their feet,
Following Thy blest example, be it called
After my name, and may the peasant folk
Utter to distant time one prayer for me,
And cry "God rest our sister's soul in peace!"*

CONSTANCE.

"Velut ægri somnia."—HORACE, *Ars Poet.* 7.

  I had—perchance I still may have—a friend.
Her name—we'll call it Constance: she to me,
For four long years,—nay, rather brief, not long,—
Was sharer of my thoughts, my hopes, my fears,—
In matters where the Muse doth dominate:
And so each day, and week, and month, and year,
My wonder grew to see how leal and sage

---

*The garden at Eisenach and its fountain and coppice-wood are still called by the peasants after the name of the "dear" St. Elizabeth.

And true was all she thought and said and did.
She shone a perfect woman in mine eyes,
Judged e'en by highest standard; my regard
For her grew more and more; tender respect
And manly sympathy in this world's woes—
(Woes that had thrown a sobering halo round
Her inmost being, and had well-nigh crushed
Her heart of hearts)—was all I had to give.
And this I gave her freely. And she said
That to my "manly sympathy" she owed
All that is priceless in this lower world,
Reason and Hope; and I had wept with her
Beside her mother's death-bed, and had sworn
That come what might of sorrow, pain, or grief,
I would be her true friend.

       I never thought
To steer my bark upon the Tropic seas
Of Love, so full of storm and sudden squall,
But on serener Friendship's temperate waves
To sail secure; and then, methought, the while
Tempests would ne'er arise, no thunder-cloud
Would overcast the bright pure heav'n above—
The heaven that her presence was to me. [by;
Yes, so I thought, I dreamed. And months rolled
And daily at her home an honoured guest
(More honoured than I ever sought to be),
I sate beside her, and securely sate,
And watched her as from month to month she grew
Willing to visit those glad scenes again
Where once she shone the "fairest of the fair."
And then when tidings, well-nigh worse than death,
Came from a far-off land, how that her son,
Her well-loved son, had prospered but amiss,
Fain would I forth have gone and sought and found
The wand'rer, and have brought him back, and said,

"See here, thou mother dear, thy long lost son!"
And oh! had word of slight or scorn been said
Of him or her, how would my soul have fired!
How had I burned to vindicate the wrong!

 Yes! friendship is a sacred, holy thing,
Akin to love, and yet divergent far.
There can be friendship where no love may be;
And friendship can do all that love can do,
And often more besides. And when it bleeds,
It pours as red and rich a stream from out
Its side as love doth from the inmost heart.

 "Well; and this friendship lasted?"
          Many a month;
Then months went on to years; and yet it seemed
Our friendship grew more sacred than before,
Though it knew nought of love—of earthly love.
But more it did; it helped to raise me far
Above my base self—taught me, as I strove
To make me worthy of it, to aspire
To higher, nobler, more unselfish ways;
And I would put my grosser interests by,
And school my mind to take no thought of *self*,
If only I could minister to *her*.
All that was hers, moreover, soon became
Thrice dear to me; her very children's face
Remembered me of all the mother was.
Her looks were treasured in mine inmost soul;
Her thoughts, transmuted, passed into my thoughts:
In her I lived, and on her voice I hung,—
That voice that to my ear was music sweet.
The very rustling of her silken robe
Struck on my ear with no unheeded sound;
And when she spoke and greeted my approach,
She seemed to say, "Whatever may betide

" Elsewhere, at least in me you read a friend,
" And friendly welcome ever waits you here."

  * * * * *

" Well, and what then? Say, did this friendship
  last?
" And doth it prove abiding? Spring returns
" And passeth into summer. But the sun,
" The summer solstice past, sinks slowly down,
" And winter's frosts come back."
         I know it, friend;
And fool I was to deem my lot was free
From mortal change and sharp vicissitude.
For, when my sun shone brightest, and the sky
Was bluest and serenest in its depths,
No bigger than a human hand, one cloud,
One little cloud, upon th' horizon seen
First indistinctly, lowered, and lowering grew,
Till it obscured my heaven. Then all grew dark
And dizzy round my head; I swooned and sunk
Fainting and prostrate on th' unpitying ground.

Then earth and earthly things or passed away
Or seemed to pass; the sunless atmosphere
Chilled the dull life-blood in mine inmost veins;
I passed into oblivion: day by day
I lay upon the ground or on my couch
Half wandering, half oblivious. Sleepless nights
And days of slumber passed upon my brain,
My giddy brain; and oft and oft I prayed
In mercy God would take me to Himself,
Nor lengthen out th' unwelcome boon of life.
And when at last I slept, I dreamed a dream:
(Was it a dream?)—I wandered by the brink
Of silvery Thames, and a kind eye looked down
Upon me, such as once was Constance's;

And then it grew so solemn, stern and fierce,
I fled affrighted; and I knew no more,
Save that I thought I heard a gurgling noise
Of waters round me, and beheld the blue
And bright ethereal depths beneath the stream
Of that swift river as it glided by,
And woke in other worlds—a suicide.

  My sleep it passed, and with it fled my dream:
And then I knew what narrow bound had stood
Betwixt me and my madness.
                        "And what means
"This hair-breadth 'scape? this sad foretaste of
    woe?"

  I know not, and I cannot yet divine.
I served her faithfully, and Constance knows
I served her faithfully, sought not mine own,
Thought not mine own, nor ever strove to climb
The lofty "pedestal" on which she loved
To place her worshipp'd heroes.
                           I perchance
Did falsify her high-wrought hopes of me.
Sooth I was never made to stand admir'd
Of all beholders; and I shrink the gaze
Of those who upward look to me. A place
More humble and more lowly far be mine.
But this I know; God be my witness here!
I never thought to wrong her, and I ne'er
Wrong'd her by scornful thought, or word, or deed.
I would have laid my life down on the sand,
And sacrificed my veriest hope of heaven,
To light the load of her enduring grief.
And I would do so now. Though storms have ris'n
To overcloud the brightness of my sky,
Yet ready am I once again, renewed

In health, and strength, and life, to vow **myself**
Her manly, tender, sympathetic friend.
Her name is " **Constance.**" I will ne'er believe
That **she** can have **forsworn that** virtue which
Her name remembers. **Oh! that** she would say,
As **once** she said, " Dear friend, I look for you ;
" Will greet **your** advent as I used to greet.
" Come **to the** old familiar haunts, and talk
" **The old** familiar talk to willing ears ;
" Think the **old** thoughts, and dwell upon the themes
"That **once** were not distasteful. **See where** stands
" **Vacant the chair in** which you wont **to sit**
" In my sad days **of weary** desolateness.
"Think of **the past no** more. If clouds **arose,**
" (As thou dost say) upon thy summer **sky,**
" *I* saw them not ; nor did *I* raise the storm.
" I would not willingly fling **back in** scorn
" A manly heart's **true** friendship. Come, and **be,**
" As once we were, true and familiar friends.
" **The tiny minever who scorns to** taint
" **His fair white fleece with stain of** dirt or filth
" **Bears not a skin** more void **of all** reproach
" **Than thou in all that** thou hast done towards me.
" Thou **may'st have erred ;** that **thou wilt** freely own;
" Error **is human, and thou** art but man.
" **Forgiveness is the** woman's **noblest part :**
" 'Tis hers and highest Heaven's. Then come, nor fear
" One dark suspicion **or** reproachful word.
" The old familiar friendship **yet** shall be
" **The still familiar friendship.** Life's sad bane,
" Pride, **only pride, I know,** doth keep thee back !"

   Oh ! could **she say** these words, then swift as thought

Once more I would return. Estrangement then
Should find no place; all should be perfect peace.
Life is too sad, life is too short, for strife;
Peace only is eternal. But perchance
All this is but a dream; for mortal life
Is made of shadows, not of substances.
And if life's self be nothing but a dream,
Must not our petty strifes, our puny cares,
Our selfish interests, and our fancied wrongs—
As e'er the greater doth include the less—
Be after all but "as a sick man's dreams?"

FRIENDSHIP; AN IDYLL.

> " Felices ter et amplius
> Quos irrupta tenet copula."—
> — HORACE, 1, Od. xiii.. 18.

A five years' friendship; then a sudden pause;
Mysterious silence, unexplained offence;
A grief that cankers and consumes my soul.
Such, sister, is my story; such my fate:
A weary waiting through long wintry months
For the returning of the May-tide beam.
I wait, but wait in vain: it comes not back.
Say, is it perished wholly, while I sit
And ponder through long days, and longer nights
Lie tossing on my fever'd couch, and dream
Of happier hours that into distance dim
Are waning, or perchance are wanèd quite?
What means it all? Canst thou the riddle read,
Of this estrangement, this bewildering change,
Sweet sister? Is, then, Friendship but a name,
An idle name, a mockery and a jest,
A toy for men to take up and throw down
As some new fit may seize them?

FRIENDSHIP; AN IDYLL.

       Out upon
The cursed idea! Foul traitor him I hold
To faith, love, chivalry, **and** loyalty,
Who deems in thought, or with false lip avows
Friendship **can die** a death **and** be as though
It ne'**er** had **been**. What hath been, ever is,
And still remaineth. In man's inmost heart
There are no sands whereon to write the word
And **leave it** to the waves to **wash** away.

 Methinks, as in the golden harvest-time
When the glad reaper, eager for the sheaves
That hold the yellow treasure of his plains,
Goes forth with sickle arm'd **into** the tilth,
Then, entering, darnel finds and stubborn **tares**
Confused and mingled with **the** rip'ning grain,
And cries " an enemy hath done this thing :"
So too on friendship's fair domain, some tongue,
Some cruel, sland'rous tongue, foul seed hath sown,
To choke the golden treasure which thereon
We hoped to gather, **and part** friend from friend.

 " Nay, brother, give **not way** to sad despair.
Who **loseth** Hope, doth the sheet-anchor lose
Of **very life**; **nor** lose not Faith : have trust
In time, **in God,** and in thyself have faith.
Thou didst not speak amiss when said thy tongue,
" The vows of friendship are not writ **in** sand."
But fierce convulsion in earth's heaving breast
Will change her pleasant surface for **a** time,
Be it or short or long, and will blot out
All that is passing fair, then leave behind
A desolate blank where once **a** garden smiled.
Who knows when next or Alp **or** Appennine
Shall quake with fierce upheaval? when **or how**
Skiddaw's tall crest be shaken **to its base** ?

But Constance knows such is not Friendship's law.
Then, brother, deem not all is wreck'd and lost.
Have trust in God and in thy better self,
Thy consciousness of utter rectitude.
Time is a kindly deity ; time doth test
With power more subtle to discriminate
All that is noble, great, and good of heart ;
But shows the base man in his villainy
Naked and stripp'd of virtue's borrowed robe :
And—time will do *thee* justice in the end."

GROWTH AND PROGRESS.

A Prose Thought in Poetry.

Festina lentè.

It seemeth to the keen observant eye
That nature's growth is silent, gradual, slow ;
And 'tis a fix'd law of this lower world,
Yea, and, it may be, of the Universe,
That littlest are but parts of greater things.
The grass that decks the glad field doth not spring
By bold eruption suddenly full-grown,
But riseth by an increase so unseen,
So gentle, and so noiseless to the sense,
As may disturb no angel's ear ; may be
Invisible even to celestial eyes.
The rain it falleth not from airy clouds
In ponderous masses, but in quiet drops
Earth-ward distill'd, or subtler far descends
In breath-like moisture of refinèd mist.
Nay, and the forceful planet doth not leap
Bounding from where his orbit starts to th' end,
But ever foot by foot, and line by line,
Circles the heavens through which he wends his way.

So, too, the mind of man by process slow
Works out its silent ends all secretly;
Intellect, feelings, habits, character,
Are gently moulded as by hands unseen
Until they reach their perfect end and aim,
By slow advances and by lesser steps
Grown to full stature.
      So in morals, too,
Yea, and in Faith, it is by lesser things
That act upon us or whereon we act,
By small resolves that seem of no account,
Do we make up the total of our growth
This way or that; and each of mortal men,
Feeling and finding, half unconscious, walks
That onward path which in its latest stage
Shall bring his steps to Heaven or lowest Hell.

RIENZI: A DIALOGUE.

These lines, it is proper to inform the reader, are a paraphrase of the eighth chapter of Book I. of Bulwer-Lytton's novel, Rienzi.

ADRIAN, RIENZI.

R. Thou wrongs't me, Adrian, thou dost wrong me. I
 Play not the part of a vile demagogue,
 Nor seek to stir the depths of popular will
 To skim therefrom the uplifted lees of fortune.
 Long have I brooded o'er the past; so long
 I seem to have grown a part of it; to have wrought
 My soul to own one master-passion, to see
 Old Rome restored to all her ancient glories.

A. Say, by what means?

     R. My Lord, one only way
Lies open to restore a people's greatness;
'Tis through the people's heart : to *them* appeal.
No princes, nor no lords can make a state
For ever glorious; they but raise themselves,
Drag not the people up along with them.
Trust me, the people must work out their own
New birth to glory.
     A. Nay then, have we read,
Or you or I, history amiss. Methinks
'Tis the scant few, the mass regenerate,
And what the few work straight the mass
   accepts.
But let us not dispute, as in the schools
Men wrangle, taking now this side, now that.
Thou say'st, dear friend, a crisis is at hand,
That the "Good State" shall soon be 'stab-
   lished? How
Where are your soldiers? Where their arms?
   say, are
The nobles now less strong than heretofore?
And shows the mob a face more bold, more firm?
Heaven knows, I speak not with the prejudice
Of a mere noble-born. I weep with tears
The long debasement of my country's cause.
I am a simple Roman : in that name
I do forget my loftier birth. But yet
I dread the storm you heedless raise, dear
   friend.
Say that you raise it,—violent it must be;
Purchased maybe with blood, the blood of those
Rome holds most noble. Ye will aim to drive
Them, like the Tarquins, forth your gates; but
   see
Ye rouse not Sylla's day once more, and bring

Sylla's proscription **back**. Say, massacres
And like disorders, do they pave the way
To **glorious** peace? Then, if ye chance to **fail**,
The chains of Rome are rivetted for aye.
Fail in your still-born struggle to escape,
Ye give your lords excuse fresh chains to bind
On their tamed slaves.
        R. What then would ye desire?
Say shall we wait in patience till **the** day
Colonna and Orsini strive **no more**?
Say, shall we sue this lord for **liberty**
That lord for justice? Good **my lord**, 'twere
        vain
To call on nobles **to** oppose the nobles.
Like ever cleaves to like. We dare not ask
The nobles that they moderate their power.
That power **to** our own selves we must restore.
There may be, must be, danger in the effort:
But we shall make it in the Forum rich
In brave memorials of the people's cause:
And if we fall, **we** fall, right worthily
Of them who went before us. Nobles, ye
Boast high descent, **wide** lands and sounding
        names:
Ye boast **of** your ancestral honours: yet
We, too, have ours. Our fathers, **they were** free,
Though of the people sprung. **Say,** where is
        now
Our heritage? their heritage? Not sold,
Not given, I ween, but filched by slow degrees,
Filched from us while **we** slept, **or** from us
        wrung,
Amid our cries and struggles, by strong hands.
My lord, **we ask you** but that heritage.
'Tis ours, **'tis yours.** Your liberty is gone

When ours departs. Say, can ye safely dwell
But in fenced castles? Can ye walk Rome's
    streets
Unarmed at dusk or in the darkening night?
True, ye may guard ye with your swords, but
    we
May not and dare not gird them on our sides.
Yes! ye may outrage, terrify unscathed
Us peaceful citizens: but can licence bear
Fruits like to those of golden liberty?
Ye have both pomp and power; but equal laws
Sure were a safer and a nobler boon.
Were I Colonna's chief, my heart would pant
For the free air which doth surround us all,
Not through pent bars and bulwarks raised to
    hold
Our brethren in fast check. Give Heaven's
    free air:
Give us the safeguard of free popular law,
And banish foul suspicion from the state.
The tyrant deems or rather dreams him free,
As lord o'er slaves; but in free states, methinks
The meanest hind is far more free than he.
Oh, good my lord, that you, of noble soul,
Generous, enlightened, brave, alone amid
Your Peers in knowledge of true freedom's right,
With our desires would sympathise, and strike
One blow with us to vindicate our cause!

A. Then thou wouldst war upon my kinsman, say,
Of high Colonna's race?*

---

*A Prince Colonna is still the head of this historical house, and Prince-Assistant at the Pontifical Throne. There are only two Roman "Princes-Assistant," the Orsini and the Colonna, and the charge is the highest at the Papal Court and hereditary in each family.

    R.   His life, his lands,
His name is safe: we simply war against
His power to work us wrong. I am a man
He fears and hates; he sees around him raised
Castles and battlements; but *me* he sees
Strong in the hearts of Roman citizens.
Yet he and all his tribe, mefears, are blind.
Patient, I bide my hour.
    A.   What seek'st thou then?

R. I ask for safety and just laws for all.
Nor will less boon content me. Let the nobles
Pull down their castle walls, disband forthwith
Their armed retainers, so in all things stand
Equal before the laws of this great state.

A. Vain hope! Ask what Rome's nobles yet may grant.

R. Nay, if that hope is vain, I make appeal
Straight to our people's hearts. Prudence may well
Direct a thriving state; but when that state
Sinks to low death and sleeps its faith away,
Th' inspired alone can wake it back to life!
The die is cast. I will regenerate
Rome, or else, failing, in Rome's ruin fall.
May God and God's own saints defend the right!

THE LAST PLANTAGENET.

    Eastwell, near Ashford, in Kent, is noteworthy as being the burial place of one of the last Plantagenets, if not the very last, a natural son of King Richard III. This son, after the Battle of Bosworth Field, voluntarily retired into a private station, and worked, it is said, as a labourer, being allowed by Sir Thomas Moyle to build himself a cottage on the edge of his park at Eastwell. The death of this person is recorded in the parish register of burials simply and touchingly as " Richard Plantagenet, Dec. 22, 1552." The curious readers can peruse the story in fuller detail in my " Tales of Great Families."—E.W.

" I am the last of the Plantagenets :
These eyes have witness'd Bosworth's fateful field,
Where Richard fell beneath th' o'erpowering lance
Of Lancaster's Red Rose. Thence wandering forth,
Southward I fled ; the Kentish Weald I passed,
Halting where Eastwell's lord with kindliest care
Received me, offering safe retreat from those
Who fain would strike to earth a wounded prince.
There gained I leave to build myself a home,
A humble homestead on the wooodland skirt
Of a great lord's domains : for he in arms
Had served King Richard in his younger days.
And oft, ere yet the early sun be ris'n,
Stray I athwart the woodland, dig or delve,
Or 'neath the noontide beam, on labour bent,
Ply my dull spade, or drive the loaded wain.
Then next my tiny plot of tilth I sow,
Three acres barely, with a wealth of corn.
And often, while the summer sun goes down,
Climbing one high-ridged corner of the park,
Gaze seaward as I watch him slant descend
Towards the blue Sussex Downs.
                              A Tudor sits
On the proud throne of England. Be it so.
But still it lieth in the womb of Time.—
(Such is King Henry in his tyrant mood,
That vile apostate from the Church of Christ,)—
If Tudor yet shall work my country's weal.
That issue resteth in the hands of God.
His holy will be done ! Content I live ;
Content I die,—the last Plantagenet :
Last of my father's not dishonour'd line :

And, when I pass the bar and gate of Death,
May reverent hands in yonder churchyard sod
Consign my dead bones to a grassy grave,
Waiting the glorious Resurrection morn.

A PROPHET INDEED.*

(Suggested by Dean Stanley's Sermon in Westminster Abbey, June 19th, 1870, the Sunday after the funeral of Charles Dickens.)

He Who, at sundry times, in divers ways,
Hath spoke to man, Who in the former age,
Spake by His prophets and apostles, spake
To all men by His Christ, still sheds His gifts,
Diverse in kind, yet all in harmony.
To each He giveth of His own to hold;
He giveth to the Muse her poesy;
Giveth to orators their eloquence;
Giveth to science its deep scrutiny
Of things that lie pent in old Nature's womb;
Giveth to moralist and preacher wit
To point a lesson to his fellow man.
Yet in these latter days one gift of gifts,
Greater than each, greater, maybe, than all,
He pours abroad, the blest dramatic power;
Imagination, fancy to conceive
And—far more wondrous—genius to create
The fiction'd character, to limn the form,
The manners, actions, and strange ways of thought,
Of men who live not, e'en as though they were.
So Shakespeare's wit, and Milton's inner gaze
Into mysterious space, from God came down;
And Scott, thy pictured tales of chivalry,

---

*It is scarcely necessary to remind the classical reader that the word 'Prophet' in Greek signifies as often one who speaks and teaches publicly as one who foretells events beforehand.

That soften, teach, enoble, humanize;
All were to ye the precious grace of Heaven.

Nor less His gifts, who, 'neath the Minster pile—
(That centre and fond heart of English love),
Now rests and slumbers.
      He, with soul and pen,
Fired by diviner power than e'er he dream'd,
Taught high and low the lesson of the Christ;
Taught men the holiness of poverty;
School'd roughest natures into tenderness;
Taught us to weep with them that weep, and joy
With those that joy; taught us the pure, the true,
The loveable, the merciful, the good;
Taught us to read the lineaments of God
In each poor outcast—in the pauper child
To know a fellow-heir of highest heaven.
 Say, was he not a "prophet" in his age?
Say, knit he not the bonds of human love—
The ties of sympathy 'twixt man and man
That hold across wide-intervening seas?
Strange power? mysterious gift!
        And cometh not
Each good and perfect gift from Him alone,
The great Creator, Who is "Love" itself,
Who made, and keeps, supports, and loves us all?

SHENSTONE AND COWPER.

Yes! the Leasowes* are charming, and he who
  created
That sweet pretty landscape deserves to be fêted;
But I scarce can allow him, at least if I know it,

---

*The Leasowes is the name of Shenstone's seat in Shropshire.

The divine and adorable name of a poet.
He is pretty and graceful, and highly refin'd;
But where is his verse that shows genius of mind?*
His " streams " never dash over rocks, but, alas!
All dull and prosaic " meander " through grass:
His shrubs are all trim, and, right properly placed,
Decorous they range on each side of the waste:
His flocks are correct in their conduct, and play,
Like good lambkins, in sunshine, and frisk all the
    day;
And, that his surroundings may all be in keeping,
Like his bees, so his verses,"invite one to sleeping."†
In his stanzas melodious and soft is no fire,
But he twangs and he twangs his monotonous lyre,
Raising " vales " where each " swain " sits and
    " pipes " on a " reed,"
Thus transporting the Po to the banks of the Tweed,
Or rather of Avon: but where is the Muse
Like his who sang nobly on banks of the Ouse?
The Muse of our Cowper, true psalmist of nature,
Who bade us uplooking to know our Creator?‡
Who cared little for fame and for earthly renown,
Taught that " God made the country," while " man
    made the town ";
Who pictured each field and each woodland and
    grove,
And all sweet rural joys:—he the poet of love
Domestic and homely, the poet of peace
And religion, whose voice cried to slavery," Cease"!

---

*Ingenium cui sit, cui mens divinior, atque os
Magna sonaturum, da nominis hujus honorem.
　　　　　　　　　　　—Horace, I Sat. IV., 43, 44.

†" My banks they are furnish'd with bees
　Whose murmurs invite one to sleep."

‡" Look up through nature unto nature's God."

Who wrote what he felt in the depths of his heart,
Own'd no master but God, and could ne'er play a part;
And regardless of either man's smile or his frown,
Was content with the mantle that Milton threw down.

ON THE QUEEN'S JUBILEE VISIT to the CITY, 1887.

" The Queen! the Queen! joy to the city be!
" Wave, wave, ye flags! deck the gay streets:"
        perchance
Thus to veneer the city's front, and hide
The secret sufferings of our patient poor,
Is well for days of jubilee. What know
Eyes royal of the seamy side of life?
Behind that parti-streak'd Venetian mast
Begirt with bunting and with flowers bedeck'd,
From slow starvation dies a weary man,
His wife and children following to the grave.
There lies a toiler, worn by long disease,
That with a thousand pains his limbs hath rack'd,
And left him crippled till his youth be fled.
Little *they* reck of gladness. Not for *such*
Loud bells ring out in thunder-peals of joy;
Not for *them* beats the drum: no branches green,
With roses and fair woodbine intertwin'd,
Dispel the sad gloom of their prison-house.

This should not be. T'was " Merrie England " erst;
God grant she may be "merrie" once again!

THE OLD PILGRIM'S DEATH.

It was a stranger pilgrim; and he came
In age extreme to Erin's sainted shores;

For that a vision told him while he slept
That, should his due feet stray to Shannon's stream,
He yet should hear once more those bells so sweet
Which cheer'd his youth, on which long months of
    toil
He spent, ere yet his country fell a prey
To fierce invaders, and God's convent, sack'd
Rose up in smoke to heaven.
                      Then lost he all,
Home, hearth and friends, went forth a wanderer,
North, south, east, west, an exile upon earth,
And passed long years in weary pilgrimage.

    "And this," he cried, "is Shannon? tell me,
        friends!
"That I may lay my bones in peace beside
"His sacred flood. Now, now, I know full well
"Kind death is near at hand. Once more I hear
"Those bells that chime so sweet. Adown the
    stream
"Nearer and nearer sound they. Oh! t'is joy,
"Joy of my youth now lengthened out to age.
"I see, I see the city fair my dream
"Sweetly forshadowed, and I know the voice
"That kindly calls me homeward. Let me die
"Beside the waves of Shannon's friendly tide."

    He spoke and crossed his hands and lips and
        brow,
And blest the day on which to his glad ears
Were wafted sounds that spake of southern home;
Then turned his face toward the holy cross
That crowns the tower, and mov'd his lips in prayer.

      *   *   *   *   *

    But ne'er those lips shall move in prayer again;

Kind death hath claim'd the pilgrim as his own,
And call'd the wanderer to his home in heaven.
God grant him rest and peace, his journey o'er!

"MY LIBRARY."*

My Library to me is Kingdom large enough.—SHAKESPEARE.

" A Kingdom large enough for me,"
Writes Shakespeare, " is my Library."
See : all ye fairies, sprites, and elves,
What scores of volumes fill my shelves,
Old and familiar friends, 't is true :
I love them all—and so should you.
" Well, what their names ? and what their ages?
And do you read the pleasant pages
Written by all these reverend sages "?
  Some I have read, not all I fear :
Some I will try to read next year ;
And mean, when I the time can find, to
Master each one that I've a mind to.
  First Shakespeare comes, the grand old poet,
Foremost and chief—all people know it.
See how he stands a prince to view,
Nature's own priest and prophet too ;
The child of fancy, bard of truth,
Idol alike of age and youth :
Yes : place as long as you may live, sir,
To him, as to the ladies, give, sir.

*The above lines were recited by me in 1889, at the end of a lecture on " Readers and Reading," which I delivered at the opening of some Classes for mutual self-improvement, in the Schoolroom attached to one of the Nonconformist chapels in Marylebone.]

Next Milton, with the seraph throng
Of Paradise shall join his song,
And tell how Eden, lost by sin,
Man in the later days shall win.
Then the old tale shall Byron tell
That youths and maidens love so well ;
" Childe Harold " and the " Grecian Isles,"
Italian scenes and Spanish smiles.
Then wizard Scott shall wake anew
The muse that sung of " Rhoderic Dhu,"
" Megg Merrilees," and " Ivanhoe,"
" Marmion," " the last old Minstrel's Lay,"
" The Lady of the Lake," the day
When Flodden saw proud Scotia mourn
Her monarch slain, her banners torn.

  With these a few of lesser fame,
Yet worthy of the poet's name ;
Pope, Wordsworth, Cowper, here be seen,
And Longfellow's " Evangeline."
Landor and Coleridge, Spenser, Gray,
Southey and Rogers, Goldsmith, Gay,
Campbell and Burns shall bear the bell
With Keble, Hemans, " L.E.L."
Here Tennyson enthroned shall bring
His " Princess," " Idylls of the King,"
With wholesomest rebuke declare
The pride of " Lady Vere de Vere,"
And tell how nature changeth " ever "
Her face in all things save " the river,"
Or welcome in the May-Day Queen,
To crown her on the village green.

  See Johnson's wisdom all is there,
Pourtrayed by honest Boswell's care.
Then " Nights Arabian " greet the eye
Of boys and girls right welcomely ;

Thackeray is there, Macaulay too,
Ainsworth, George Eliot, meet my view:
Food for grown fowls and younger chickens,
Mine eye rests pleasantly on Dickens,
While childhood's memory bids me tell   [Nell."
Of "Smike," "Squeers," "Twist," and "Little
"Gamp," the "fat boy of Dingley Dell,"
And all those scenes with pleasure rife,
Of stage and town and country life.
Bunyan the preacher needs must be
Added to this grand company,
The mind with holiest thoughts to leaven,
And point the "Pilgrim's path to heaven."

Freeman the Conqueror's tale shall tell,
That story which he lov'd so well;
The Greece of Thirlwall and of Grote;
All that Froude, Hume, and Lingard wrote;
The victories strange o'er nature won
By Layard, Burton, Livingstone,
Speke, Stanley; all that Ruskin says,
Chief "Master" of these latter days;
Here on my shelves shall treasured be,—
A great and glorious company.

Two names* excepted, poets, sages,
Historians, "heirs of all the ages,"
Too many to be told, I fear,—
Yes, one and all, are welcome here.
They crowd my shelves. You can't do better
Than read them to their latest letter.

---

*I refer to Robert Browning and Thomas Carlyle, neither of whom seem to me able to write plain honest simple English, and who must therefore, I fear, be hopelessly unintelligible, and therefore useless, to the average English reader.

LIFE'S HARMONY; MAN AND WOMAN.

Suggested by Lytton-Bulwer's " Parisians."—*Book II. Chap. vii.*

Her level aye let woman keep. She stands
Nearer, it may be, to her husband's heart,
For that she raiseth not her woman's head
Equal to his diviner height. 'Tis thus,
In music and in poesy, there rules
A dominant note, and out of this, we see,
In combination with the weaker sound
Doth perfect harmony arise. Just so,
The greater to the less, the strong to the weak,
Wedded, conjoined, make this world's harmony,
Which over-strained equality doth kill.
  Not all her gifts doth nature give to both:
Diverse to man and woman. He for strength,
She made for grace and beauty. Daring he
And confident of purpose; weaker she
And diffident. In action great is man,
Woman in suffering. Man may shine abroad,
Woman gives light at home. Man to convince
Strives, gentler woman seeks but to persuade.
Man's heart is rugged; woman's tender, soft;
He toils life's evils to prevent, which she
Burns to relieve. Science is man's domain,
But taste is woman's. Judgment he may boast,
She sensibility; stern justice he;
But tenderer mercy is the woman's sphere.

BEAUTY.

Suggested by Lytton-Bulwer's " Alice."—*Book II. Chap. i.*

Oh! beauty, beauty! for thou art twice blest;
Thou blessest him that gazes rapt on thee,

And thou dost bless thine owner. Sure thou art
At once th' effect of goodness and its cause.
A loving soul, a disposition sweet,
A nature loving and affectionate,
Speak in the very eyes, the lips, the brow,
And give its birth to beauty's self. We view
A fair face and we straight admire. There is
In such a sight more than the vulgar dream.
Beauty, thou 'rt sure a treasure sent from heaven!
To gladden each dark chamber in our hearts.
From heav'n thou com'st, and heav'n is thy true
    home.

BEPPO; Stanzas for Music.

It is customary in rural districts of Italy and in other parts of Southern Europe to encourage village contests in singing, a small laurel crown or other trifling reward being given as a prize. The custom is as old as the days of Virgil in Italy, and those of Theocritus in Sicily.

  Hark! afar the merry bells are ringing;
Nearer, hark! are merry voices singing;
See! glad youths and rose-crowned maidens,
    bringing
  Forth the rustic hero to our hall.

Down the vale glad notes of song are swelling;
Down the street wake joyous echoes, telling
How thy song, all other songs excelling,
  For our rustic prize aloud doth call.

Comliest of all village swains, we greet thee!
Thine the muse, and thine the crown we mete thee;
Sing thus ever, Beppo, we entreat thee;
  For thy skill in song outstrips us all.

TO E. BASTARD, Esq., OF KITLEY.

Lines written at the Land's End, 1851.

I stood upon the far-most western cliff
   That frowns upon the blue Atlantic sea,
And ever and anon my heart returned
   To thine ancestral hall and dwelt on thee;
Dear friend, whose tender sympathetic heart
Can melt at other's woes and bear in them a part.

And as I gazed on that fair scene, a prayer
   Once and again I breathed to heaven most high,
That He who rules the boisterous winds and waves
   Would deign to guide aright thy destiny,
And give his angels charge thy bark to bear
Safe o'er the perils of old ocean's war.

Oh! may the tides that lash these rugged shores
   Smile on thy peaceful course across the deep;
And may thy guardian angel hovering near
   Watch by thy side, nor turn aside to sleep:
And Mary mother, with her looks of love,
"Star of the sea," bear succour from above.

TO THE BIRDS ON A RETURN OF SPRING.

Oh! be joyful, be joyful, ye children of Heaven,
   The glad days of spring will be with ye ere long;
Kind nature will warm all the buds into blossom,
   And bid each gay bosom to burst into song.
Joy, ye birds in your nests, and with winter's departure
   On St. Valentine's eve keep your spousals so gay;
Bnt remember that March winds and April's cold showers
   Must pass ere ye joy in the sunshine of May.

And then for our selves, as the days they grow longer,
  And the skies brighter shine, while ye carol and sing,
Let us e'en press this thought to our hearts and remember
  "It takes more than one swallow to make up a spring."

THE POET'S WALK.

Thrice envied is the poet's lot in life;
The graceful vision of old Nature's face
He sees and joys to see; to him her smile
Doth smile indeed: and when 'mid lonesome wilds,
Bleak moors or russet hills, o'er mountain tops,
He toils his way, he doth not walk alone.
On snow-clad Alps, on glorious Appennines,
On sunny shores of Menton's bright blue sea,
Where voice nor sound is heard, save lowing kine,
Or bark of honest watch-dog, shepherd's song,
Or voice of muleteer; the stones cry out;
The solitude speaks to his inward ear
Long pent in heart of city or of town.

LINES SUGGESTED by W. S. LANDOR'S DECAMERON; "DANTE & BEATRICE."

Tis said that in the pure and serene air
That round the higher peaks of Alpine snow
Circles, when years have sped, once-living forms
All fair and beautiful in death are found
Like flies preserved in amber. So methinks
Virtue all fresh 'mid th' ambient air of life
Lives on, and, saved from death's damp charnel-house,
Gives forth her grateful odour to the sky.

AN IRISH EVICTION AT CHRISTMAS.

Homo homini lupus.

What is that I heard ye singing?
   Say, oh say those words again:
"Glory be to God the highest!
   Peace on earth! Good-will to men!"

Oh! those words of bitter satire!
   Oh! the irony of life!
Oh! those cruel sounds that barter
   Peace **for** war and love for strife!

Hear **the voice of** famished London!
   What was that the workers said—
Fathers, mothers, sons, and daughters?—
   "Give us labour! give us bread!"

But the voice in accents louder
   Rises from **old** Erin's shore,
"Spare us, we are helpless; spare us!
   Give us life; we ask no more."

Cross, oh! cross, the stormy Channel;
   Hear the wild sad Irish cry:
"**Give us food, and** laws, and justice!
   Give us **freedom or** we die.

"Break the chains that bind us **to ye**!
   From your fetters set us free!
Deem **us** serfs and slaves no longer!
   Give us life and liberty."

"Peace **on earth!**" evictor **cruel!**
   Bid those mocking words **to** cease!
"Tear **the roof** from off yon hovel!
   Lay it waste, and call it peace!*

---

*"Solitudinem faciunt, pacem appellant."—TACITUS.

"Down with wall and down with rafter!
    Hack the stone, and tear the thatch!
Drive into the wilds each inmate!"
    Well such deeds your words bematch!

What? "Good-will to men?" I ask ye,
    Christmas crowbars, what they mean?
Mark the hill-side, bare of heather;
    Mark the crouching forms between!

Irish brother! Irish sister!
    Though across the seas ye wander,
"English house is English castle,"
    "Sauce for goose is sauce for gander!"

Is the Celt a slave or freeman,
    Dwell he far or dwell he near?
Say! are homesteads, poor and lowly,
    Are they sacred only here?

Beat not Irish hearts as warmly
    As the heart of Saxon hind?
"Tenant!" "crofter!" "cottar!" rouse ye!
    Claim the rights of human kind.

"Tenant!" "crofter!" "cottar"! "slaveling!"
    By whatever name ye're known,
"Be not like dumb driven cattle;"
    Claim that hovel! 'tis your own.

Ireland's soil! Though lords usurp it,
    Yours a share by law and right!
Strong in God's own strength, resistless
    They shall find a nation's might.

"Idle!" "wild!" "rebellious!" "lawless!"
    In our nostrils stinks your name;
"Thriftless!" "worthless!" "slaves, and beggars!"
    Yes! But whose the guilt and shame?

Tell the tale of devastation ;
  England knows not half your story ;
English hearts will beat with Irish
  When they read your deeds of glory.

Ireland's sons are brave and noble ;
  Ireland's daughters chaste and pure.
We have robbed ye, we the Saxon ;
  We have driv'n ye from your door.

Ours the guilt. Bad laws we gave ye ;
  We will for those laws atone.
We will give ye back your freedom ;
  Ireland shall be all your own.

"Peace on earth !" once more I witness
  Commerce, justice, laws and learning,
Banished long from town and village,
  To old Erin's shores returning.

Yes ! a better day is rising !
  O'er your hill-tops gleams the light ;
Gladstone's voice, by England echoed,
  Drives afar the shades of night.

Till the soil in hope ! the darkness
  Doth but herald in the dawn.
Till the soil in hope ! 'tis coldest
  Close before the break of morn !

Till the soil ! your land shall flourish
  Once again from sea to sea :
On the Liffey's banks your leaders
  Soon shall cry " Uprise, be free ! "

Once again I see ye prosper
  On your shores of Emerald green :
One the tie that binds ye to us :—
  Ireland's pride is England's Queen.

THE HOUSE OF LORDS.

The House of Lords! The House of Lords!
   Say, shall we " mend " or shall we " end " it?
To terminate the House of Peers
   Really, good Sir, we don't intend it.

We want a trifling change to see
   In the fixt mode of their election;
We want the principle affirm'd,
   Just now, of " natural selection."

When next our Queen proclaims her will
   That her dear " cousins " straight be sent
To counsel her on matters grave
   In her " High Court of Parliament,"

Let her refuse to summon those
   Who for law-making have no care,
Peers who will neither " toil nor spin,"
   And really " have no business there; "

Peers who disgrace their honour'd names
   In public or " beneath the rose,"
Live dissipated lives at clubs,
   And figure in the Courts as " Co's."

Bid careless Lords to stay at home,
   Devote their time to cultivation
Of wheat, of turnips, peas, and beans,
   For which, perchance, they've some vocation;

Give up all share in making laws,
   Severely leave alone the " masses,"
Resign their votes, if not their seats,
   And herd among their selfish " classes."

Yes, Queen! Create life-peers by scores,
   Or, at the very least, by dozens;

Grant no hereditary rights
  To your new-manufactured cousins.

The House of Lords! The House of Lords!
  To Home Rule's cause we must convert them;
Slow work 'twill be, but slow is sure;
  The Lords themselves, we would not hurt them.

They'll vote all wrong, I know for years,
  Indulging in long fruitless sitting;
But really Sarum's noble lord
  Should school them to give way when fitting;

Unless they wish to see, forsooth,
  Honours and titles of to-day,
Along with England's ancient crown,
  In some vast deluge swept away.

OUR NEW PREMIER; LORD ROSEBERY.

(From a Primrose point of view.)

Say the Tories, "Thank God, now he's ruined the land,
We are rid of "the old Parliamentary hand;"
Though, if aught is still left to be ruined, Lord Rosebery
Will soon follow his steps and be "playing old gooseberry;"
But the "Primrose" Clubs surely should know that young Turk
Himself after all is a Primrose†—see Burke.

---

†His Lordship's titles, according to Burke's Peerage, are Earl, Viscount, and Baron Rosebery, Baron Dalmeny, Viscount Inverkeithing, and Baron Primrose. His family name also is Primrose.

THE CURSE OF MEG MERRILIES.

(See " Guy Mannering."—Chap. viii.)

Ride on, Ellangowan ! go, ride on your way !
Ye have quenched seven hearth-fires in ruin this day ;
Ride on in your pride, Ellangowan ! I wiss,
Will the fire in your parlour burn brighter for this ?

Ye have e'en torn the straw from our rafters ; but see
If that thatch will add strength to your ancient roof-tree :
Ye may stable your stirks in the huts at Derncleugh ;
See the hare doth not crouch on the hearth-stone with you.

Ride on, Ellangowan ! why gaze ye afar
At the exiles ye've driven to strife and to war ?
Not a soul 'mongst our clan but would fast one and all,
So laird Bertram ne'er wanted a sunket in hall.

See the fifty puir souls ye have drove from their bields,
To sleep with the brock and the tod in the fields,
With the lav'rock, the hern, and the black-cock to bide,
And to roam with the wild grouse along the moor side.

Ride on, Ellangowan ! we're weary, but aye
We will carry our bairns, though we faint by the way.
Ride on in your pride ! but while roofless we roam,
Go see your braw cradle be fairer at home.

May your bairns live and prosper within your ha' door,

And may God give them **hearts** that are kind to the poor.
And schooled by life's sorrows, and purged in the fire,
Better folk may they prove them than Bertram, their sire.

Ride on, Ellangowan! ride proud and ride fast:
The word that I speak it shall e'en be my last—
The last till the young laird come back to his ain,
And a Bertram shall hold his **brave** castle again.

"THREE ACRES AND A COW."

"Two sons of the soil, incited, no doubt, by recent promises made to them by the Candidates, took to the polling-place, when they went to vote, a halter a-piece, expecting each to be presented with a cow. The presiding officer was somewhat surprised at being asked by one of the rustics if they might make their choice among the cattle of a neighbouring park."—*Life*, 1885.

I have heard you speak of "three acres of land,"
With "a cow" to belong to each peasant band;
Tell me, oh! where are those acres found,
That promised spot of domestic ground?
Tell me, oh! where is that happy shore
Where we all shall settle, and starve no more?
   Not here, not here, **my boy**.

Where father shall sit 'neath his sheltering **vine**,
And smoke his **own** pipe, **and** drink his wine,
While mother **and** sisters, **at tea in** the shade,
Bless the rosy bowers their hands have made;
And the cow untethered, **and** ranging free,
Crops the summer wealth of **our** acres three?
   Not here, not here, **my boy**.

Say, **are** they then where rich travellers roam

O'er the heathery hills of the " Scot at home ? "
Or are they where Erin's gay sons abide,
By the Liffey's stream or the Shannon's tide ?
Or are they in Northern or Southern Wales,
Where St. David's cliffs woo the western gales ?
    Not there, not there, my boy.

Eye hath not seen them, my gentle Will,
Ear hath not heard of them ; valley or hill,
Pasture, or moorland, or woodland fair,
John Hodge and his brats may not settle there ;
For the acres belong to a landed swell,
Who loves his own property far too well ;
    Not there, not there, my boy.

Trust not, oh trust not, a statesman's smiles !
These visions so fair are delusion's wiles,
For the cow is "the cow" that "leaped over the
    moon,"
When "the dish ran away" with the fabled "spoon,"
And the acres are only " *Chateaux en Espagne*,"
Built up in the head of Joe Chamberlain ;
    They are there, they are there, my boy.

THE EXECUTION OF VAILLANT.

February 5th, 1894.

" So Vaillant's gone."   Gone whither, friend ?
    I'm really half ashamed to ask it.
His soul, let's *hope*, to God : his head
    Has fall'n into the traitor's basket.

A fitting place for such as him,
    Foul murderer of fair liberty ;

The base assassin of his own,
    His country's vilest enemy.

Curs'd be the man, whoe'er he be
    By blood or birth, who rais'd his hand
Broadcast to scatter Death and deal
    Destruction through his native land!

For this, you know, he would have done,
    (Fair France, methinks, will ne'er forget him),
But one small thing prevented him,
    High Heav'n would never, never, let him.

Milton, the poet regicide,
    Smil'd on the Whitehall tragedy
Approval (God forgive the deed!)
    But sorrowed when he came to die.

Grand words he wrote that live and breathe
    Inspired in grand prophetic mood,
" Licence they cry, not liberty,
    For who loves *that* is wise and good."

Sure if e'er freedom had a priest
    'Twas Milton; and what Milton wrote
I, as a humble " Liberal " scribe,
    Am not ashamed this day to quote.

England, beware! In " Anarchist "
    Th' assassin lives, th' assassin thrives:
He simply wants to waste your homes,
    Rob your dear children and your wives.

England, beware! go, ask your Queen
    On bended knees for equal laws,
For equal justice, equal rights,
    But ne'er give up the grand old cause!

PERFECT PEACE; WRITTEN IN ILLNESS.

"Thou wilt keep him in perfect peace whose mind is stayed on Thee."—*Isaiah xxvi.* 3.

O Thou, Whose hand can still the waves,
   And bid their tulmult cease,
Give me Thy faith, Thy daily grace,
   And with it—perfect peace.

Oh Thou Whose power can calm and check
   Each tumult of the soul,
O make me feel Thy presence now;
   All evil thoughts control;

And when his darts assail me most,
   Bid the foul fiend to cease;
But in that last dread hour of death
   O give me—perfect peace.

KYRIE ELEÏSON.

When our souls are sunk in woe,
As we wander here below,
When our tears for sin would flow,
                Kyrie Eleïson.

When we lie in doubt and fear
As the hour of death draws near,
And thy summons, Christ, we hear,
                Kyrie Kleïson.

When the Tempter would assail,
And, dreading lest his blast prevail,
On our tossed bark we shorten sail,
                Kyrie Eleïson.

When our limbs are racked with pain,

And our struggling eyes we strain,
And our prayers seem most in vain,
Kyrie Eleïson.

When we draw our latest breath,
Though its parting lingereth,
When our eyes are glazed in death,
Kyrie Eleïson.

When before Thy throne we stand.
There to hear the dread command,
May we be call'd to Thy right hand,
Kyrie Eleïson.

THE GIFT OF TEARS.

Grant me, O God, the precious gift,
   The sacred gift of tears,
To purge mine inmost soul from sin,
   And chase away my fears;
Oh! that my tears could flow for Thee,
As Thine, Good Lord, did flow for me!

Yes! at the grave of him, His "friend,"
   Remember, "Jesus wept,"
And Thou didst in the Garden weep
   While Thy companions slept:
Oh! that my tears could flow for Thee
As Thine, Good Lord, did flow for me!

TRANSLATED FROM
AN OLD ECCLESIASTICAL POEM.

Natu Dei felix homo collætatur fratribus,
Misellinis et pupillis egenis et orphanis,;
In his sæpe susceperunt viri celsi Dominum.

The birth of God taught happy man to feel

A gladsome sympathy with all mankind,
With lepers, orphans, and with those in need :
By helping such, great souls have put on Christ.

NAZARETH.

"Can aught of good rise out of Nazareth?"
Come, doubter, come and see. In this poor town,
So scorn'd of all, a bye-word and a jest,
Worketh the lowly art of carpenter
The Son of Mary and of Joseph—He
A child, observant of His parent's will,
Albeit the hidden Lord of heaven and earth.
His home a cottage 'twixt the grassy down
And turfy hillside and the saltless sea.
His seat a workright's bench : so passing fair
With child-like smile, His fingers toil and moil,
If thus He may increase His parents' store ;
So poor, though sprung from Judah's royal line,
So passing poor : and yet in Him there dwells
The fulness of the Godhead bodily.

Scorn we not humble things ; lest ignorant
Of good, the good escape us. Oftentimes
In lowliest guise, in pilgrim's garb may be,
We entertain an angel unawares.

THE ORDER OF St. JOHN.

Star of eight points ! well thou remembrest me
Of words divine, once uttered on the Mount
By Him who never spake as speaketh man.
Blest are the poor in spirit, they who mourn,
The meek and pure of heart, they who do thirst

For righteousness, the merciful, and they
Who make for **peace, they who** for God's own **sake**
Do **suffer persecution and endure**
Lies **and revilings, nor in turn revile.**

" *Pro Fide* " is our motto, and our faith
Is faith not **void of works ;** a faith world-wide,
That in its universal Charity
Knows **no** distinction or of **creed or clime.**
To **work man's good in spirit** of that **Faith***
St. John **doth school us ;** in his star we shine.
Kings be our fathers, Queens our nursing mothers ;
While Princes joy to bear upon their breasts
Th' eight-pointed star, the badge of good St. John †

THE BEATITUDES PARAPHRASED.

" Blest are **the poor in** spirit, **for to** them
Belongs Heaven's Kingdom ; Blest are they **who**
       mourn,
They shall **be comforted ; yea ; Blest** the meek,
They shall **be this world's heirs ;** Blessèd are they
Who hunger after righteousness ; their lips
Fillèd shall be. **Blest** are the merciful ;

---

*The second motto of our Order—(I write "our," for **I** rejoice to say that I am **one of its** oldest members)— is " *Pro utilitate hominum.*"

†In **1888** Her Gracious Majesty Queen Victoria consented to become the Sovereign Head and "Patron" of the Order of the Hospital of St. John of Jerusalem, **and** H.R.H. the Prince of Wales was installed as its "Grand Prior." At the same time or within a year **or** two afterwards, **their Royal Highnesses** the (late) Duke of Clarence and the Duke **of Y**ork, the Empress Frederick of Germany, the Princess Mary **Adelaide of Teck, the** Princess Frederika of Hanover, and all **or** nearly all **the members of** our Royal House, were admitted into **the Order,** whose badge is worn by them, including Her Majesty, **at all** Drawing-rooms and on other public occasions.

G

To them shall mercy come : ye, pure in heart
Are Blessèd, in the vision of your God.
Blessèd the peacemakers : they shall be called
God's children ; Blest are they who for the sake
Of justice persecution shall endure :
Theirs is Heaven's Kingdom. Blest are ye when men
Revile and torture you and falsely say
For My name's sake foul lies of every kind
Against you. Then rejoice ye and be glad ;
Great your reward in heaven ; so this world's sons
God's prophets heretofore did persecute."

DAVID PARAPHRASED.

(1) Psalm xc., verses 9-10.

When thou, Good Lord, art angered, all our days
Are gone : Straight to their end we bring our years,
E'en as a dream or tale that sick men tell.
The days of man are three score years and ten ;
And though men be so strong as that they come
To four score years, yet is their aged strength
But labour and but sorrow. Thus so soon
Passeth our life away, and we are gone !

(2) Psalm xxiv.

The earth and that within its bounds doth live,
Is all the Lord's ; to Him its compass broad
Belongs of right and they that dwell therein ;
For on the seas and floods He founded all.
Who shall ascend into God's holy hill,
To that bright place where He in glory dwells ?
Whoso hath clean hands and heart purified,
Who doth not unto vanity uplift
His mind, nor hath his neighbour with foul lies
Sworn to deceive. This servant from his Lord

Shall aye be blessèd in His righteousness;
For God is his salvation. Such His face
Do seek in earnest, and their race is blest.
Lift up your heads, ye gates! be ye lift up
Ye everlasting doors! See enter in
The King of Glory; strong is He in truth,
And in the battle mighty. Lift your heads,
Ye everlasting doors! He enters in,
The King of Glory and the Lord of Hosts.
Bow low your heads; in adoration, bow!
Ye angels and ye spirits of the just.
Who is the King of Glory? who, but He?
The Lord of Hosts, the Lord of Hosts doth reign.

(3) Psalm cxx.

When troubles came about me, then I called
Upon the Lord, and He did hear my voice.
"Deliver me from lying lips, good Lord,
And from deceitful tongues. What recompence,
Say, shall be thine, false tongue? E'en arrows strong
And mighty, and hot-burning coals of fire.
Woe, woe is me, that I perforce must dwell
In Mesach's bounds and in false Kedar's tents.
Too long my soul hath dwelt among sworn foes
Of peace and of my life. For peace I've strove;
But when I speak of peace they straight prepare
Warfare malignant. Lord, how long, how long"?

ON THE DEATH OF A BELOVED SISTER,
AT BRIGHTON, DEC. 16, 1844.

Yes! thou wert pure, my sister, and for thee
  Did the world spread its flattering toils in vain;
  For thou did'st walk unharm'd, though sin and pain
Around thy path stood leaguèd constantly,

Summer and winter season, night and day,
  Whiles thou did'st even keep the tenor of thy way.
Yes! thou wert pure and saintly in thy death;
  Unspotted from the world, thou did'st pursue
  The peaceful paths of life, and, heaven in view,
Meek to thy Maker's hand resign'dst thy breath,
  Who, as He did thy waking thoughts engage,
  Closed in serenest calm thine earthly pilgrimage.
The one chief solace of a father's heart
  While age rolled on and fell the wintry snow
  Of threescore years upon his whitening brow,
Whose in his breast but thine the larger part?
  Thou wert his loved one once, and thou art flown
  To regions happier far, and we must weep alone.
Alone, forbid the thought! e'en while we sigh,
  And call thee " poor," forsooth, and drop the tear
  Of sad affection on thy funeral bier,
Perchance thou 'rt smiling as thou standest by,
  Unseen yet not unseeing, and dost throw
  One pitying glance of love on this dull home below.
Take then this tribute; and, if e'er 'tis given
  To sainted angels' pure and hallowed breath
  To hold sweet converse with this world beneath
As down they gaze from their blest seats in Heaven,
  Teach us in faith to kiss the chastening rod,
  Which smites us but to draw our cold hearts nearer God.

THE SLEEP OF THE FAITHFUL DEPARTED.

Lines Suggested by the same Event.

Say, shall we mourn the mighty dead,
  We creatures of a day,

And mourn around an empty coil
    The soul hath cast away?

We knelt and kneeling scarce could hear
    The slow pang of distress;
While o'er her features stole the hue
    Of a faded loveliness.

So mute her pale and feverish lips,
    So free from earthly care;
Well might we muse and fondly dream
    An angel slumbered there.

Silent she lay; then, " Mercy, Lord "!
    " Father in Heaven "! she cried;
" Receive my soul for Jesu's sake "!
    Sank back and calmly died.

Then mourn her not, our sister dear,
    For death is chang'd to sleep;
Not for the happy peaceful dead
    But for the living weep.

Yes! weep for us who journey on
    Life's dark and dreary road;
What falls and perils e'er we reach
    That blest and bright abode!

Thus, when from life's dim prison-house
    Death comes to set us free,
Oh! let our hearts be fixed above,
    Nor fall, good Lord, from thee.

TO MY GUARDIAN ANGEL: MORNING.

Guardian Angel! thou hast kept
Watch around me while I slept:

Free from harm and peril now
With the cross I sign my brow;
Risen with the rising sun,
Forth I go, but not alone:
For, my keeper and my guide,
Thou art ever by my side.
Pour then ever in mine ear
Words which angels joy to hear;
Curb thou my tongue and thoughts within,
And keep my wandering eyes from sin;
And rule my steps along the road
Which brings me nearer to my God.

 Glory to the Father be,
Glory, Jesus Christ, to Thee,
And Holy Ghost, Eternal Three.

TO THE SAME: EVENING.

Holy Guardian Angel: keep
Watch around me while I sleep;
'Neath the shelter of thy wings,
Save me from all hurtful things;
Pour the light of love divine
On this cold dull heart of mine;
Evil spirits drive away,
That I may rise at break of day
Again to praise my God and pray.

 Glory to the Father be,
Glory, Jesus Christ, to Thee,
And Holy Ghost, Eternal Three.

THE INFANCY OF JESUS.

Jesus, Thou wert meek and mild,

Thou wert once a little child.
Lo, a little child, to Thee,
Saviour dear, I bend my knee:
Make me gentle, mild, and meek.
Teach me, Lord, Thy face to seek.
  In a manger Thou wast born:
Jesu, teach Thy child to scorn
This world's riches and with Thee
Live content in poverty.
Once in Nazareth's humble cot
Thou didst taste of childhood's lot,
And while summers rollèd on
Thou wert reared as Joseph's son,
Son of the humble carpenter,
Though of high heaven and earth the heir.
Pure thou wert from taint of sin,
For the Godhead dwelt within.
Him Thou didst obey and her,
Mary, Thine own mother dear:
Blessèd above women she,
Blessèd above all in Thee!
On Thine infant face meanwhile
Oft she shed a mother's smile,
As she joyed to look upon
Thee her first and only son.
Virgin mother! ever blest,
Mary, teach me on thy breast
With thy Jesus there to rest.
Mother, keep me meek and mild,
Keep me with Him for thy child,
That, Jesus, I may live to Thee
In holy Christian infancy.
And as on each year doth flow,
Teach me still in grace to grow;
Teach me ever to obey,

Never from Thy steps to stray;
By Thy cross and precious Blood
Make me holy, chaste, and good;
Bow my will that when, at last,
Christian childhood may be past,
I may love and serve Thee too,
And in heaven Thy sweetness know.

SUFFER the LITTLE CHILDREN to COME UNTO ME.

I think when I read that sweet story of old,
   When Jesus was here among men,
How he called little children, like lambs, to His fold,
   I should like to have been with Him then.*

Yet why should I think He's no longer on earth,
   When He says, " I am all days with you "?
For sure, if He loves little children like me,
   Then his words must be simple and true.

No; He cannot deceive. His dear mother I'll call
   And straight to His altar repair;
For they say He still dwells in that sweet holy place,
   And an infant may worship Him there.

THE HOLY TRINITY.

When God's dear Son came down and dwelt
   A man upon this lower earth,
The heavenly choir proclaimed Him nigh,
   And " herald angels " sung His birth;
Then may I join their notes divine,
And make their hallowed raptures mine?

Yes; for I am a Christian child,

---

*The First Stanza is not original.

I am not as the heathen are;
And blessèd be God's heavenly name,
　His mercy and His grace I share:
And so with angel powers above
I too may sing and praise His love.

Yes; for that God who sent His son
　On earth, He is my Father too;
He washed me clean when born in sin,
　And bathed me with baptismal dew;
God's priest be crossed and signed my brow,
And so God is my Father now.

Yes; for God's son came down to save
　From sin and death the world and me,
And Jesus for His brethren died
　A sacrifice on Calvary;
I am His brother, and His blood
Brings little children nigh to God.

Yes; for he hath sent down on me
　The comforter and Fount of love,
His holy Spirit—and sheds His grace
　On all God's children from above,
To dwell and reign our hearts within,
And keep our infant souls from sin.

Yes; for through life all praise and love
　To Thee, great Three in One, I owe;
And all God's mighty works of grace
　A little Christian child may know;
For God hath taught His Church, and she
Reveals them one by one to me.

She tells me how a Virgin pure
　The mother of my God became;
She bids me call her mother too

And fondly lisp her sacred name:
Yes; from His cross He gave us thee
Our mother, Mary dear, to be.

Then will I serve this gracious God,
   And strive to love Him more and more,
And thank Him that He deigns to shed
   His gifts in such a boundless store;
And, if I love Him, I shall see
In Heaven a glad eternity.

HOME.

Oh! how I love you, father dear!
   I love my mother too;
I've none within this happy world
   One half so dear as you.

Sisters and brothers, each in turn,
   Share all my joys and fears:
Oh! what a bright glad home is mine!
   This home of smiles and tears.

But then you tell me I have got
   A dearer Home above,
A scene where sorrow enters not,
   A home of peace and love.

For worldly joys, though bright they shine,
   Come quick, and then decay;
And parents' love and earthly smiles
   Of home soon pass away.

What though I have a father here,
   That father hath been given
To lead my infant heart to love
   Our Father dear in Heaven.

And mothers' love, so fond, so pure,
  Oh! what is that to me,
As often as I think upon
  The love that dwells in thee.

Mary, dear mother of my Lord,
  So blest, so "full of grace,"
Oh how I love to look upon
  "The brightness of Thy face!"

Thus all I see on this glad earth
  Faint types and shadows are
Of joys that fade not in the sky,
  That home so bright and fair.

A THOUGHT ON CREEDS.

A few short simple truths, I vow,
  Suffice for all the Church's needs.
Oh! when shall God's hand cut atwain
  The enmities of rival Creeds?

GEMS FROM CLASSIC MINES.

NO. I. CHORUS FROM THE "KNIGHTS" OF ARISTOPHANES.

King of the main, Poseidon, hear!
God of the earth-born steed, appear!
For well, I ween, thou lov'st the neigh
And brass-rung hoof of courser gay:
Lov'st thou to see each azure prow
Glide swiftly o'er thy waves below:
To thee, great king, in gladsome sport
At Athens' race our sons resort;

For thee the toilsome contest bear,
For thee the flower-wove chaplet wear.
God of the golden trident, now
A 'very present help' be thou:
Joyful our chorus bids thee come
With welcome to thy spray-dashed home.
Adored on Sunium's rocky height
Thou seest the sportive dolphin play;
Gerestus' cliff proclaims thy might,
Who on thy Phormio smild'st amid the battle fray:
Arise! if e'er, be present now!
Arise! and hear our suppliant vow!

NO. II. PROPERTIUS, IV. ELEG. XXI.

"*Magnum iter ad doctas proficisci cogor Athenas.*"

I'll hie me to some distant shore,
To Athens, seat of learned lore;
For other climes may chance to heal
The rankling wound this breast doth feel,
While on my mistress' brow intent
More and more keen my soul is bent.
Sickened, each cure in vain I try:
What boots earth's best philosophy?
Can rules of sages calm this breast?
Ah, no! the God forbids me rest.
One only cure, one balm remains;
I'll hie me to far distant plains
O'er the blue seas, and banish there
From soul and thought the phantom fair.
   Come, comrades, ply your oars, your sail
Spread willing to the western gale;
The salt wave wantons round me now,
The sea-breeze fans my burning brow:
Ye fading towers of Rome, adieu!

Farewell, ye friends so fond and true;
Farewell each vale, each hill, each glade,
And fare thee well, deceitful maid.
The surge of Adria's stormy bay
Bears me but further on my way
To that fair land where hearts are true—
Where all is old, yet all is new.
I cross the blue Ionian wave,
Those waters that glad Hellas lave;
Flashes Piræus on my sight;
I see, all bathed in glorious light,
Walls which shall live for aye in fame,
And still record their Theseus' name.
See how around that ancient pile
Halos of glory seem to smile;
In Plato's garden, lo! I sit,
And revel in Menander's wit;
Or thoughtful roam through learned groves,
And meditate on hopeless loves;
Or list in mute and fond suspense,
Demosthenes, thine eloquence;
Then, lingering in long galleries,
With pictured heroes feast mine eyes,
Or, pondering in bewildered maze,
On living statues stand and gaze.
These be my joys, till, fleeting by,
Age dims my sense, and dulls mine eye.
So, Athens, shall thy sunny clime
And long-drawn interval of time
Soothe life's decay, and when I die,
Honoured shall live my memory.

NO. III. SOPHOCLES, FRAGMENT.

Goddess fair,—beware my son!

Venus hath more names than one.
She is Heaven, and she is Hell,
She is might invincible ;
She is lust and strong desire,
She is fiercely madd'ning fire ;
She is joy, and she is gladness,
She is woe, and she is sadness ;
She is gentle, wrathful, good,
In her ever changeful mood :
Rest she knows not ; night and day,
Who is not her constant prey ?
In the scaly tribe supreme
Rules she 'neath old Ocean's stream ;
Gods beside their nectar lying,
Sorry mortals, daily dying,
Beasts of earth all stoop to her,
Feather'd fowls of highest air.
Witness Heaven! the Queen of Love
Rules tyrant in the breast of Jove.
Yes, she ever hath controll'd
Those of more than mortal mould ;
And if Heaven she conquers, then
Vain the strife of mortal men.
Thrice the contest we essay,
Thrice we rue th' unequal fray ;
Recks she trusty sword nor shield,
In sevenfold armour dight we yield :
Then " mercy, spare us, Queen of Love ! "
Cry men below and Gods above.

NO. IV. HORACE, III. ODE, IX.

HORACE.

While I was lovely in thine eyes, and yet
  None other youth preferred to me did throw

Round thy fair neck his arms, happy I lived :
   The Persian monarch no such bliss did know.

LYDIA.

Long as none other maiden shared thy heart,
   Nor Chloë shone preferred to me, the while,
With name illustrious as the Vestal maid,
   Ilia, by thee proud would I sit and smile.

HORACE.

Now Thracian Chloë holds me in fond chain,
   Fair queen of verse, mistress of melody ;
If but the Fates my soul will spare, for her
   Fain would I live, for her I fain would die.

LYDIA.

I too can love ; and Thurian Calaïs
   Inflames my bosom with congenial fire :
If but the Fates will spare the youth I love,
   Twice would I mount content the funeral pyre.

HORACE.

What if our ancient love once more revive,
   And with fond link two hearts rebind amain ?
If auburn Chloë from my hearth be spurn'd,
   And injur'd Lydia cross my doors again ?

LYDIA.

Though he is brighter than the noonday sun,
   Thou light as cork, and fickle as the sky
That smiles on Adria's waves, with thee alone
   Fain would I live, and fain with thee would die.

NO. V. HORACE, I. ODE, XXXVIII.

Boy ! I detest your Persian feasts,
   In vain for me their garlands bloom ;

Search not where smiles the lingering rose
   Ere yet it meet its wintry doom.

Be Paphian myrtles all thy care ;
   They well become this flowing wine :
They best befit the Bard, reclined
   At ease beneath his arching vine.

NO. VI.   ATHENIAN DRINKING SONG, FROM CALLISTRATUS.

Gaily I'll wreathe my sword in myrtle bough,
   As erst Harmodius and his comrade brave,
When they gave Athens equal laws, and sped
   The tyrant to his grave.

Dearest Harmodius! sure thou art not dead,
   But wand'rest through the Islands of the Blest,
Where roams Achilleus, brave, and swift of foot,
   And Tydeus' son hath rest.

Then gay I'll wreathe my sword in myrtle bough,
   As erst Harmodius and his friend so true,
When at thy feast, great Pallas, they conspired
   To make the tyrant rue.

And ever shall thy name in story live,
   Dearest Harmodius, with thy comrade brave,
Who gave to Athens equal laws, and sped
   The tyrant to his grave.

NO. VII.   FROM CATULLUS.

  As safe from ruthless herds and hinds there blows
In charming solitude a fragrant rose,
Called forth by dews, by suns made fair and strong,

By gales refreshed, **pride of the** summer throng,
It flowers; each blooming **maiden** sounds its praise;
On it young shepherds with **fond** wishes gaze.
But **if the flower** be ravished from its bed
By some proud **spoiler, and in** ruin spread,
No blooming **maid is lavish** in its praise,
No youthful shepherds **with fond** wishes gaze.
So, **while** the fair **one** lives all chaste and pure,
She smiles, and sweet love hovers round her door;
But when the **bloom** of purity is lost,
Her faded **honour is an** empty boast:
She falls unknown—she charms no suitor's eyes,
And mid her comrades fair, unpitied dies.

NO. VIII. VIRGIL, GEORG. II. 532,—40.

Thus rustic ran the ancient Sabine life:
This life both Romulus and Remus lived;
So grew **the brave** Etruscan **state,** and so
Rome burst her cradle, grew earth's pride, and girt
Queenlike her sevenfold hills **with** wall of strength.
T'was thus ere yet the Cretan monarch reigned;
Ere yet man's impious race the horned steer
To heaven would sacrifice, then **feast amain**
By th' altar's base; and such "**the golden** prime"
Of Saturn upon earth: nor yet **was heard**
The trumpet's blare; nor on the anvil's edge
Would fierce swords echo back the puissant stroke.

NO IX. VIRGIL, GEORGIC III. 349, &c.

Anon, where Scythian hordes **the sea** surround,

And swollen Ister rolls his tawny waves,
And Rhodopè high towers in Northern skies,
The shepherd keeps his steers within their fold.
No verdure clothes the field, no leaves the trees;
But huge unsightly heaps of snow deep driv'n
O'er-canopy the land seven ells in depth.
Eternal winter holds her icy reign.
Scarce the slant sun scatters the shades of night
At early morn-tide or at sunset hour.
There splits the brass with frost; stiff grows the robe
E'en on men's shoulders, and th' erst liquid wine
Stands solid, as the ditches in the field,
And axes cleave it; and long icicles
Hang from the beard all frozen to the ground.
Ice-fields form sudden on the rippling brook:
The wave that erst the sailing barque would skim
Now bears upon its back the broadest wains.

NO. X. FROM W. S. LANDOR'S "CANUM TRIUM SEPULCHRA."

Farewell! ye faithful hounds: Kind Demiphon
To ye a place of sepulture hath given
Midst pleasant glades and gardens, where he walks
With due feet, and long may he tread these paths!
Oh! may I sleep like you, dear faithful friends,
Far from the foul haunts of a faithless tribe
Of liars! Gracious God: to think that such
Thrive and abound, while ye with earthborn worms
Mingling your dust, rot in forgotten graves!
Say then, doth justice live?

NO. XI. FROM PROPERTIUS.

All things on which our senses dwell by day,
When sunk in slumber kindly night brings back.
Laid on his dreamy couch, the huntsman's soul
In sleeping hours the woodland toils recalls,
And hears his vocal hounds. To courts of law
Judges in dream revert ; his chariot-wheels
Live present to the driver ; nightly steeds
Bear him in sleep along the fancied course.
Me too the Muse 'neath night's all-silent wing
Visits in sleep, and stirs my soul in rest.

PART II.

MISCELLANEOUS, HUMOROUS, EPIGRAMS, &c.

MY EMMA AND CUPID.
(From "Once a Week.")

"No earthly love my path shall cross,"
Romantic Emma cries; "Love's dross;
And hearts are foolish empty toys,
For moon-struck maids and sillier boys.
No! happy in my single state,
I'll live and die without a mate."

Sly Cupid heard the fair maid's vow,
And, chuckling, drew his amber bow,
Then whispered in mine ear, "My friend,
"Fear not, this whim will find its end;
Fair Emma is not what she seems,
And when a young maid vows, she dreams.
I swear by these unerring darts,
I can read maidens' inmost hearts;
And what is true of A.B.C.
(Not to say anything of D.)
Can scarce be false of E.F.G.
Trust me, your Emma means but this,—
Should some fond lover steal a kiss,
Standing upon her left or right,
She'll not let slip the lucky wight,
But *do her best to hold him tight!*"

I'VE A NOTION.

Rhymes read by me, as "ye Rhymer," before the members of "ye Sette of Odd Volumes," at their monthly festive gathering and dinner at Willis's Rooms, King Street, Jan. 6th, 1887.

Ye Rhymer is painfully solicited by his daughter, Laura, to rhyme one or more New Year's Fyttes. Ye Rhymer, however, writeth sarcastically, and discourseth painfully, as well he may, for his experiences of life, and especially of domestic life, have been somewhat sad and bitter.

FYTTE THE FIRST: RES DOMESTICÆ.

Well, Papa, since you're sixty this coming July,
And have seen, read, and thought a great deal, will you try
To summon up some of your old recollections,
And give me your "notions" with sundry reflections?

Well, Laura, I'll try. I've a notion that home
Is a spot from which wise men will seek not to roam;
That its innocent joys and its pure recollections
Are the only true source of domestic affections.

I've a notion there's little indeed in a name;
That Jew, Christian, Turk, Heathen, are all much the same;
That those by your side who in trouble will stand,
You may count on the fingers of only one hand.

I've a notion that love is a dangerous game,
I've a notion that wedlock is mostly the same;
I've a notion that paint is preferred now to beauty,
That too often self-interest banishes duty.

I've a notion that curls of hair, like unto gold,
Are a snare and delusion, in Regent Street sold;
That girls' faces are masks, and that honest intentions

Are a part of H—'s pavement, or simple inventions.

I've a notion that mannikins, mashers, and such
Are in favour with women, French, English and Dutch;
That men's candour and honesty, honour and truth
Are regarded as merely weak symptoms of youth.

I've a notion that wives are not saints in disguise,
And that history's self is a packet of lies.
I've a notion we're all in a bad sort of way
When the question is only "will this or that *pay?*"

I've a notion we all have far too many cousins,
That 'twere well to reduce them from scores down to dozens;
And I think that life's load would be largely improved
If these plentiful "cousins" were all "once removed."

I've a notion, too, Laura, though uncles are glorious,
That the habits of aunts* are distinctly censorious;
And that 'twill be but fair in a far other sphere
To pitch into those aunts who have lectured us here.

I've a notion the Court of Divorce will not fail
On our nobles and gentles to levy black-mail;
To bear yearly crops of sin, scandal, and crime,
From now to the uttermost end of old Time.

I've a notion that as to this Court of Divorce
The *Pall Mall* gives reports, *in extenso*, of course,
For Stead fears the weak vessel, Madame, how they'll hammer her

---

*Ye Rhymer here ventureth to express a modest hope that he may not be thought in any way to assail or to question anything that Sir John Lubbock may, or may not, have written on " The Habits of *Ants*."

If such matters are heard by the judges *in camerâ*.

On this score 'tis not easy to please every pater—
Familias, I fear, and still more every *mater;*
For as soon as a paper such naughty things retails,
The young ladies, like Eve, *will* pry into the details.

I've a notion that, while there are " Potiphars "
    plenty,
You will scarcely find even one " Joseph " in twenty.
I've a notion that schools are scant teachers of
    knowledge
Which youths mostly forget when transplanted to
    college.

I've a few other notions. For instance, I think—
Take a horse to the pond, but you can't make him
    drink ;
So the forced restitution of conjugal right, Sir,
I hold is not easy by day or by night, Sir.

I've a notion that weddings and funerals too,
And christenings are anything rather than new ;
I've a notion that women are weak, men are strong,
And that sermons are terribly stupid and long.

I've a notion there's truth in defining a widower
As " a man who is awfully glad he is rid o' her ; "
I've a notion that summer 's the season for ices ;
I've a notion that Gladstone's the man for the crisis.

I've a notion that gratitude—is it not rum ?
Is a lively discernment of favours to come ;
And a friend truly grateful, when eyeing your store,
Is only an " Oliver asking for more."

FYTTE YE SECOND: RES POLITICÆ.

[Here ye Rhymer will perchance be found to run counter to ye opinions of many brethren of ye Sette, for which he humbly sues pardon aforehand.]

I've a notion of Bogeys the greatest just now
Is Home Rule; it kicks up such a terrible row;
And that, fail it or no, still, however that may be,
The truest Home Ruler of all is—the Baby.

I've a notion that Tory opinions " won't work ";
That the Christian is scarcely as good as the Turk;
That a turnip can boast that it's "always consistent;"
That the Liberal innings are not very distant.

I've a Jubilee notion—don't think me a fool—
Fifty years are too short for a good Queen to rule;
But to bad queens and kings I would give shorter range,
Though I fear a bad Sovereign's not easy to change.

I've a notion Queen Anne is as dead as King John;
I've a notion that " two eyes see better than one;"
I've a notion that kisses are sweeter than blows;
That 'tis better to vote with the ayes than the noes.

I've a notion three men, though in earnest, *are'nt* able
To " settle Home Rule as they sit round a table;
I've *no* notion at what sage resolve they'll arrive
When this conclave's augmented from three men to five.

I've a notion a Whig's much the same as a Tory;
That the " ins " and the " outs " seek for pelf, place, and glory;

I've a notion—O pray do not think I am joking !—
The Income Tax* *is* most intensely provoking.

I've a notion that politics are but a sport ;
I've a notion the Queen should be more at her Court ;
And should *I* be elected for Fiddle-de-Dee,
I think I should make a most useful " M.P."

I've a notion that wages are terribly scant now,
That our labouring poor are too often in want now ;
I most gladly would help them ; but still I *do* think,
Though they've little to eat, they take too much to drink.

" As drunk as a Lord " was a phrase in the youth
Of our fathers and grandsires—perhaps with much truth ;
But I seldom have seen a Peer swilling away
Like some few working men on this last Boxing Day.

In fact I've a notion it *is* a great sin
For our toilers to waste so much money in gin,
And that if to themselves they would only be true,
To improve their own lot is a thing they could do.

And yet I've a notion our Guardians should find
Relief-works for those who to work have a mind.
Hunger 's sharp to the poor, though it 's sauce to the few ;†
And " Satan finds work for hands idle to do."

Still I hold it *is* wrong, when our town population
Cries for labour and stands on the brink of starvation,

---

*Since these lines were written the Income Tax has been reduced by Sir W. Harcourt in favour of the less wealthy classes.
†Optimum condimentum est fames.

To be guilty of making such terrible flukes
As buying for thousands Murillos from Dukes.*

FYTTE THE THIRD: DE OMNIBUS REBUS ET QUIBUSDAM ALIIS.

Ye Rhymer discourseth, somewhat ramblingly, on numerous topics of the times, very many of them of a literary and scientific character; therefore he falls down and here especially invokes the assistance of Apollo and the nine **Muses.**

I've a notion that gas has too long ruled our night,
And soon must give way to electrical light;
That balloons will, ere long, find some well-managed
    wings,
And ruin our railways and those sorts of things.

I've a notion that goose is not bad in September,
That a turkey is best towards the end of December;
I've a notion that whisky, or gin, if it's handy,
Is a far better thing to "top up with" than brandy.

I've a notion that "Massage" is nothing but friction,
I've a notion that few things are worse than
    "Eviction;"
I've a notion the "Blues" are no worse than the
    "Yellows,"
I've a notion "Odd Volumes" are very good fellows.

I've a notion that wide is a Usurer's maw,
I've a notion that Equity differs from Law;
That evil may sometimes be good in disguise,
That the sea-side's the parent of health and of—lies.†

---

*Ye Rhymer referreth here to ye costly purchase of sundry pictures from among ye heirlooms of ye Duke of Marlborough at Blenheim, for ye use of ye National Gallery.

†Oh! My prophetic soul! This was written four years before "Ye Rhymer" removed to Ventnor.

Though freebooters, highwaymen, foot-pads, at last
Have come (God be thanked) to be things of the past,
They don't lack successors and sure never will—
The foot-pad lives on in the publisher still.*

I've a notion indeed—pray don't think that I mock—
That the chief of such footpads is Hellicat Hock;†
And that if in the next word he's not broiled and peppered
He'll share warmish apartments with honest Jack Sheppard.

I've a notion 'twould be a most grand thing if fate
Would cause books to spring forth from an author's brain straight;
Then our Curlls and such "varmin" sure would not be slow
To shut up their shops and clear out from "the Row."

I've a notion, in fact, 'twould be jolly fine fun
To make all the publishing herd "cut and run,"
Make a blaze of each beggarly bookseller's store,
And light up the fires of old Smithfield once more.

I've a notion a warm invitation to dine
Is a thing which it seldom is wise to decline;
I've a notion that gambling's a terrible course;
I've a notion wood pavement is bad for a horse.

I've a notion that fortune a terrible jade is,

---

*Rhymers, like poets and psalmists, are not to be held to strict logical accuracy of statement, but are authorised to exaggerate by the example of good King David, who said "All men are liars," and thus to put not *partem pro toto*, but *totum pro parte*.

†I cannot identify this name among the Publishers in the *Post Office London Directory*; so perhaps the printer has not "followed copy" as he should have done.

I've a notion it's right to give place to the ladies;
I've a notion that Hampshire's the county for hogs,
I've a notion our city's a rare place for fogs.

I've a notion if Jupiter Pluvius on London
Sends a downfall of snow, he should see his work undone
By early next morn. If they were but elective,
Our parochial Ædiles would prove more effective.

In fact I've a notion if two or three " Bumbles "
Slipping down on the pavement should get a few tumbles,
Or be fined for neglect, speedy ways would be found
For cleansing our streets and unsnowing the ground.

I've a notion our Laureate, when he was younger,
Was thought by the muses a noble versemonger;
And now that he's gone to the House called "the Upper,"
He should hand on his laurels to good Martin Tupper.

I've a notion the Derby's more real fun than Ascot;
That you never should put all your eggs in one basket;
I've a notion that Ireland we ne'er need have trouble in,
For good reason—its Capital always is Dublin!

I've a notion we'd be in a far better way
If we did not eat mostly two dinners a day;
Dined at two, or at three, made our one meal a good one,
And abstained from rich sauces, mince pies and plum pudding.

I've a notion we shall not soon see a new "Boz,"
And that Neptune's a sea-monarch "what never
 was;"
I have a notion our stage is uncommonly poor,
Spite of Irving, Kate Terry, and one or two more.

I've a notion that Gladstone at seventy-seven,
Shows no symptoms of thinking of "going to
 Heaven;"*
I've a notion *Bon Marché* is found at "the Stores,"
And that Booth and Salvationist Armies are bores.

I've a notion our Sunday is awfully dull,
That our Puritan "Sabbath" keeps all the "pubs"
 full;
And so to the crowds who would hasten to see 'em
I'd throw open the "Zoo" and the British Museum.

As to dogs—I've a notion last year they were
 puzzled
To find out why Sir Charles† said they all must be
 muzzled;
And I thought London burglars alone could be glad
To see our guards' mouths shut as if they were mad.

In fact, I've a notion dog-muzzles will soon
Disappear from this earth and fly off to the moon,
Unless they turn those that were made for our
 terriers
To "improvers of dress" for our fair ladies' derriers.

I have a notion the man (and, in fact, I am certain,)
To throw light on "Arabian Nights" is Dick Burton;

---

*This was written in 1887.
†Sir Charles Warren, head of the Metropolitan Police Force.

And though he's not **one of** our " Sette," *Ædepol**
He has sent us this evening a " a very odd vol."

I've a **notion with** feathers, **and** hatchments, **and mutes,**
Undertakers **at best are** unbearable brutes ;
I've **a** notion there's nothing **on** earth like " cremation,"
To **keep our towns** healthy, it " whips all creation."

I've a notion it's quite the reverse **of a** joke
To teach that life *must* end **in** ashes and smoke ;
Though as for **the** parsons, it must be **provoking**
To see all their **church** fees a-flying to Woking.

FYTTE THE FOURTH : VALE DICENDUM EST **CUM RISU.**

This Fytte has one merit, namely, that it is the shortest **of all.** Becoming all the mellower as he draweth nearer to his ending, ye Rhymer sayeth a good word in a good cause, appropriate to the place of meeting, if not **to** the season.

I've **a** notion that Willis's Rooms are **a** school
Where " Odd Volumes," though sage, may at times play **the** fool,†
Yet where ignorant Rhymesters with profit may dine,
And **sip** Wisdom's cup **with** the walnuts and wine.

In fact, I've a notion these **Rooms are** the place

---

*Ye Rhymer humbly asketh pardon for uttering a profane oath in Latin, his **only** excuse being **that** he could find **no** suitable rhyme in English. The " vol." referred to, **be** it here recorded, is the 10th and last **of** Sir Richard Burton's un-Bowdlerized edition of the Arabian Nights, published January, 1887.

†Ye Rhymer is reminded **by an** " Odd Volume " that **the motto** on the little books printed by " **Ye** Sette " is " *Dulce est desipere in loco*," to **which** he himself ventures to suggest another and perhaps equally appropriate reading, *Dulce est desipere in* ***Joco***."

For an "Odd Volume" dinner; it's served with such
    grace;
And I've also a notion, (I think you must know it,)
That I'm only your "Rhymer," no Bard, and no
    Poet.

In conclusion, your Oddship, I humbly beg pardon,
(With one single exception),of all I've been hard on;
Ask you each to forgive what may grate on your
    ear,
And wish all brother "Odd Vols." a "Happy New
    Year."

THE LAY OF THE FAT BOY.

S<small>EE</small> "P<small>ICKWICK</small>."

"*Joe! bless that fat boy! he's always asleep.*"—M<small>R</small>. W<small>ARDELL</small>.

Yes! I was born at Dingley Dell,
    Beside a Kentish common:
My father was, I guess, a man,
    My mother was a woman.

My father worked on Dingley farm.
    His name was William Jarvis;
Turnips he hoed; and when he died
    My mother went to sarvice.

When I came in the world, I was
    A babe of wondrous size, sir,
And for the first nine days of life
    I never ope'd my eyes, sir.

I dozed and slept, and slept and dozed,
    They thought I'd never waken;

But on the tenth day when I peep'd,
   They found they were mistaken.

The nurses said "that child can't live,"
   They thought themselves so clever;
The bets were two to one that I
   Would doze and sleep for ever.

They sent me to the village school,
   Of course to learn my letters;
I simply shut my eyes and snoozed,
   And left *them* for my betters.

I sported on the village green
   Among the geese and ganders,
And round the pig-styes and the ponds
   I played my "gerrymanders."

Then mother died, and I was put
   To old Squire Wardle's stable;
But learn to groom a horse, good Lord!
   That's what I ne'er was able.

The servants call me "awkward Joe,"
   But I sit still and snore, sir,
And if they "drat" me one and all,
   I slumber on the more, sir.

If aught goes in the harbour wrong,
   I quickly can diskiver;
If Jingle hugs the "maiden aunt,"
   I *don't* sleep on for ever.

I care for nought on earth but grub,
   My fleshly tastes to pamper,
And when my master gives a feed,
   Don't I watch by the hamper?

Sometimes I'm on a message sent,
  Or else to post a letter;
D'ye think I haste on such a job?
  No! trust me, I know better.

I shut my eyes and gobble on,
  But as to waking?—never!
I know all's right at Dingley Dell,
  So I sleep on for ever.

The "parlour" it may ring for coals,
  " Missus" may sit and shiver,
Sally may call and Jane may bawl,
  But I sleep on for ever.

"Come Joe! now Joe!" the servants scream :—
  "Oh, no, as I'm a sinner."
" Gracious, they've rung and rung again."
  " Well, they may wait for dinner,

" Till I have finished this here pie
  " Cook gave me—No! I never
" Leave off till the last morsel's done;
  " I will eat on for ever."

MY NEW ARM CHAIR.

These Lines, which are intended to immortalize a certain easy chair of walnut-wood, presented to me as a New Year's gift by my old friend, Mr. Walford Selby, of the *Public Record Office*, are supposed by some persons to have suggested to Miss Eliza Cook the first idea of her well-known and touching verses entitled " The Old Arm Chair."! The supposition, I need scarcely add, is quite groundless.

I love it; I love it, and who shall dare

To chide me for loving that new arm chair?
I shall cherish it long as a worthy prize,
And shall sit in it free from tears and sighs,
For 'tis bound by a single strong band to my heart;
It came from a friend—was not bought in a mart.
Would ye learn the spell? well, sit down there,
For a pleasant seat is my new arm chair.

'Tis a present, a present; I gaze on it now,
And I think in my musing mood "as how"
Its donor, if justice were justice, should be,
In the " P. R. O." at the top of the tree.
For in private life he's as good as gold,
And a public servant of worth untold;
Yes; 'tis Walford Selby that gave me,—There!
Don't tell the Marines!—my new arm chair.

I sit and I look at that chair with joy,
For the donor I knew both as man and boy,
And I well-nigh trembled to think what fate
An old Ightham's rightful heir would wait,
When he grew and came to be thirty or more,
And I was a long way past three score.
But he's loyal and true as ever; and there
He'll live on to doom's crack in my new arm chair.

Oh! say, is it folly? What? deem me weak,
If a tear of gratitude dews my cheek,
When I sit 'twixt its arms and take my rest,
And quaff the liquor I love the best?
For 'tis made of walnut, and " got-up neat,"
And soft cushions of silk adorn its seat,
And I trust our tom-cat never will tear
One dainty tassel of Selby's chair.

"THIS IS THE LAND OF AUSTRALIA."

It is needless to state that these lines are a parody on the nursery rhyme which treats of the historic "House that Jack built." But it *is* necessary to say here that though based to some extent on fact, they refer to no single public company whatever, but are an innocent "skit" on a certain association in the city, of which the writer was himself secretary, the Board of Directors being all his own personal friends, and as honest men as London, or even England, could or can produce. The Company, as the writer can testify, was unfortunate, since it discovered that each pound's worth of minerals which it desired to raise could not be raised for a sovereign, or even for a guinea; and the company was consequently turned into a land association, in which character it still flourishes. The verses themselves were accepted by Mark Lemon for insertion in *Punch;* and with that object were placed by him for illustration in the hands of my old and and dear friend, John Leech; but his sudden death soon afterwards prevented the fulfilment of his kind intention.

This is the land of Australia.

These are the mines of silver and gold,
That lay in the land of Australia.

This is the " Mining Captain " so bold,
Who "prospected" the mines of silver and gold,
That lay in the land of Australia.

This is the gallant Companie,
Founded eighteen hundred and fifty-three,
That sent out the mining Captain so bold,
Who "prospected" the mines of silver and gold,
That lay in the land of Australia.

These are the light-hearted gentlemen,
The worthy Board of Directors ten,
Who " floated " the gallant Companie,
Founded eighteen hundred and fifty-three,
That sent out the Mining Captain so bold,
Who " prospected " the mines of silver and gold,
That lay in the land of Australia,

This is the " Gent " with his dashing pen,
Who was " Sec." to those light-hearted gentlemen,
That worthy Board of Directors ten,
Who floated the gallant Companie,
Founded eighteen hundred and fifty-three,
That sent out the Mining Captain so bold,
Who " prospected " the mines of silver and gold,
That lay in the land of Australia.

These are the lawyers with *their* " little bill,"
Messrs. Grab and Snatchem, of Diddlegate Hill,
Who " got up " and launched that companie,
Founded eighteen hundred and fifty-three
By those very same light-hearted gentlemen,
That worthy Board of Directors ten,
Who sent out the Mining " Captain " so bold,
Who " prospected " the mines of silver and gold,
That lay in the land of Australia.

These are the " venturers " rushing upstairs,
All greedy to get an allotment of shares,
In that noble and gallant Companie,
Founded eighteen hundred and fifty-three,
Controlled by those light-hearted gentlemen,
That worthy Board of Directors ten,
Who sent out the Mining Captain so bold,
Who " prospected " the mines of silver and gold,
That lay in the land of Australia.

These are a stock-jobbing lot of " bears,"
Who "rigged " the market and " puffed " the shares,
And took in the public—quite unawares—
In respect of this gallant companie,
Founded eighteen hundred and fifty-three,
While the market price went steadily down,
From fifty shillings to half-a-crown,

And the widows wept, and investors swore
They had never been done so brown before,
In spite of the Board of Directors ten,
Those honest and light-hearted gentlemen,
Who sent out the " Mining Captain " so bold,
Who " prospected " the mines of silver and gold,
That lay in the land of Australia.

This is the Court of Chancerie,
Which swallowed that ill-fated Companie,
Founded eighteen hundred and fifty-three,
Controlled by those light-hearted gentlemen,
That worthy Board of Directors ten,
Who sent out the mining " Captain " so bold,
Who " prospected " the mines of silver and gold,
That lay in the land of Australia.

This is the total dividend—*nil*—
Left after paying the lawyers' bill,
Messrs. Grab and Snatchem of Diddlegate Hill,
Who " got up " and launched that Companie,
Founded eighteen hundred and fifty-three,
Controlled by that Board of Directors ten,
Those gallant and light-hearted gentlemen,
Who sent out the Mining " Captain " so bold,
Who " prospected " the mines of silver and gold,
That lay in the land of Australia.

These are the shareholders, country and town,
Looking all of them done most uncommonly brown,
While the market price went steadily down,
From fifty shillings to half-a-crown,
As they gaze on the total dividend—*nil*,
Left after paying the lawyers' bill,
Messrs. Grab and Snatchem of Diddlegate Hill,
Who " got up " and launched that Companie,
Founded eighteen hundred and fifty three,

And controlled by those light-hearted gentlemen,
That worthy Board of Directors ten,
Who sent out that Mining Captain so bold,
Who " prospected " the mines of silver and gold,
That long lay untouched, and still lie, as I'm told,
In the far distant land of Australia.

TO LADY CLARE: VERBA NOVISSIMA.

Suggested by Tennyson's " Lady Clare."

Yes! Lady Clare! all 's straight and plain ;
   We understand each other truly ;
Plain words became an honest man ;
   I would not waste your time unduly.

So, if you'll lend a patient ear
   And listen for a little space,
I'll just recount a few plain truths,
   And hold a mirror to your face.

We once were friends : we now are foes ;
   The sin of that is not on me ;
And " there's a scar across my heart "
   That you would scarcely care to see.

You thought to bind me by a spell ;
   You thought to find me soft and meek ;
You thought to slay me with a smile
   False as the powder on your cheek.

You thought you had a captive tied
   Fast to your chariot-wheels forsooth,
That you could drag him where the fit
   Might chance to lead you—docile youth !

You thought to use me while you sat

And mourned in widowed loneliness;
My cup of manly sympathy
  You thought to drain in your distress.

And then to fling it to the ground,
  As children fling a toy away:
This was your gracious, just, return
  For honest counsels day by day!

You thought forsooth for such as me
  'Twas honour quite enough to sit
In darkened rooms and listen to
  Sallies of not the newest wit.

You thought it fair to steal my time,
  Hours, days, and afternoons by dozens:
To talk soft nonsense in my ear,
  And breathe suspicion in my cousin's.

October is the month to kill
  Pheasants, and partridges, and plovers;
You held November's darkening days
  The season fit for slaying lovers:

(Bear witness Mona's distant Isle!)
  And then, as though to make amend,
Fixed on bright April's Easter-tide
  As the best time to slay a friend.

Then, too, as though I'd lived among
  Pickpockets, knaves, and other Deuces,
You thought to lecture me betimes
  On cards—their uses and abuses.

You told me that around your friends
  You drew a mystic line—Tapù;
That if I spoke without your leave
  One word, I was no friend to you.

You thought to sow dissension, strife,
  Misunderstandings here and there,
Your victim still to mystify,
  And lead him to—the Lord knows where.

No doubt all this was "for his good!"
  No doubt with every kind intention
You drove him now this way, now that,
  And spread your toils of circumvention;

Look pleased and flattered, fawned and smiled,
  Praised the "great scholar, so profound!"
Then placed him on high pedestal
  To mock and bring him to ground.

You saw me launch my ship, set sail,
  Quit the lone port, and pace the deck;
And eager watched from off that cliff
  The little bark you thought to wreck.

I watched *you* too; and sailor-like
  Stood to my helm and cheered my crew,
Spread all my canvas out, and steered
  Wide of your clique, and wide of you.

On this side Scylla howled, on that
  Charybdis yawned, a fearful sight;
Fate taught me how to shun them both,
  And that is how I'm here to-night.

I know not how a woman can
  From friend turn "Siren"; but I'm sure
That when her age is forty-six,
  A "Siren" is at least "mature."

You were forsooth, an "utter wreck,"
  The "day of doom" had come to you,
Your heart was far away beneath

That Southern sky so soft and blue.*

Yes! there was truth in what you said,
   Though little did I dream how near
The truth you were when you confessed
   Your heart most surely was not here.

In fact you never had a heart;
   And when one day you pass where I
And you must pass, the surgeon's knife
   Will chance find out the reason why.

You are a puzzle to the world,
   And, though you may not care for pelf,
One grand enigma, mystery,—
   A riddle even to yourself.

Trust me, you much mistook your rôle;
   Your place was on some rocky isle
Luring fond seamen to their doom,
   All Circè-like to sit and smile;

Just so you coolly sat and laughed
   That cruel laugh behind your fan;
Such Clara, you opine, the meed
   Woman should pay to friendly man.

It may be so; though much I doubt,
   And when again I go to school,
Christian or Heathen, Jew or Turk,
   I'll ask my master for the rule.

     *   *   *   *   *

Yet, Clare, like me, long years ago
   You were a little child; and you

---

*The Sussex sky, when compared with that in more northerly parts of England, has almost an Italian character.
—ARCHDEACON HARE.

Once on a time—forgive plain speech—
   Lov'd what was honest, good and true.

You then would ne'er have praised or lov'd
   Ungrateful, base, perfidious brutes;
You never then, methinks, did hold
   "Kindness is due just when it suits."

You then believed, I may presume,
   "Man to his fellow man is brother,"
"Kind deeds may claim a recompence,"
   And "one good turn deserves another."

But laws like these are out of date;
   Your social code is this—" Lord love you!
Reap while you can, and where you can,
   Make hay while shines the sun above you;

Take all that you can grasp, and play
   Man as you would a tickled trout,
Caress, cajole, then turn your back
   Soon as you think he's found you out.

Say, yes, he was a useful friend,
   'Tis true, he gave me good advice;
He saved my health, faith, reason, purse;
   But—really he's no longer nice;

Seems not to care for pets like mine,
   Musicians, actors, pimps, and panders,
Bohemian hacks and nameless scribes;—
   He stares as if he'd got the glanders!

See how he sits, nor talks a word,
   How bored, dull, fidgety he looks,
Old fashioned lumber, turn him out,
   Less fit for boudoirs than for books.

And if he says a word, or asks
  An awkward 'why?' well, then, oh no!
Give reason none, sit still and laugh,
  Bid him pack up his traps and go.

My manners lack your tragic grace;
  I care not for the *Times's* thunder,
I say no bitter words of friends,
  I laugh not at my neighbour's blunder;

I like plain, honest, gentlemen,
  I care not for Bohemian livers,
Spirits abjure—cold, hot, and Home's—
  Love a plain dinner and its givers;

Speak homely truth in homely ways,
  Am kind to children, love their prattle;
Am courteous to the friends of friends,
  And turn my back on tittle-tattle;

Gloat not on scandal, will not take
  French or Italian for my type
Of moral goodness, virtue, truth,
  Smoke neither cigarette nor pipe;

Think it's as well that man should dress
  As man, and woman dress like woman,
Give all,—yes e'en the Deuce,—their due,
  Am modest, diffident, and human;

Where faults are virtues, virtues faults,
  And nought is welcome but a 'lion,'
I never wish to enter there;
  A wild beast's skin I ne'er will try on.

Inconstant Clara! 'Yours till death,'
  In your lip-language signifies
Till you have found a suppler twig

To bend and train to acting lies."

"Yours most sincerely, gratefully,"
  Means "just as long as suits my views;"
Sooth we another "Johnson" need,
  If words in such strange sense we use.

O! was it noble, was it brave,
  Or was it selfishness intense,
To shut your doors against old friends,
  Those four long years of sad suspense,

And then with tenderest cruelty,
  Me of all mortals on the crupper
Behind your pillion straight to seat,
  And bid me night by night to supper?

"I could not come too often, no!"
  You could not do without a "double,"
With patient ear for sugar'd speech,
  Kind sympathiser in your trouble.

But now I am not what I was;
  I'm vulgar, boorish, worse than bore;
Clara, if truth be so, God grant
  I ne'er again may cross your door!

Fly, Clara, fly at higher game;
  For shafts like yours I'm scarcely meet;
Slay princes, barons, counts, and dukes,
  And reign a queen in Grosvenor Street!

Reign! and when seated on your throne
  Rejoice to view the servile throng
Burn round your sofa's altar-steps
  Incence, and listen to your song—

That song which, once could charm my ear;

That song, I own, of choicest note ;
That song which, while we sat entranced,
   You poured from out your perjured throat.

Clara! you've struck one honest heart
   A mortal blow : had you your way,
All uncontrolled, relentless queen,
   Like Samson, you'd your thousands slay.

Yes ! Clara ! all is clear as noon ;
   We understand each other quite.
I'm a true, loyal, hearty friend ;
   You're a vile flirt, and so—good night.

ST. PETER AT THE GATE OF HEAVEN.

(An Ancient Legend Modernized).

St. Peter sat at Heaven's high gate,
   The keys were rattling in his pocket ;
A stranger came to enter in ;
   The saint proceeded to unlock it.

" But, first," he said, " please, let me know
   What is your claim to enter here ?
This place is only meant for them
   Whose woes on earth have been severe."

" I've tasted sufferings, on my word ;
   Goods up to London town I've carried
From Richmond twenty years, I vow ;—
   And what is more, I long was married."

" Good soul, come, enter ; there's a place
   For you, but on the lower benches ;
The higher seats are all reserved
   . For doubly-wedded youths and wenches."

Another soon arrives. " Well, now,
   What is your business? Quick, declare it."
" I have been married twice; indeed,
   'Twas **very, very** hard to bear it."

" Come in, good **friend**; **step** up, until
   You find that you can climb no higher;
You've drank your drain of sorrow's cup;
   You've had your purge of earthly fire."

" Two wives! Good Heav'n! to think of that!
   Well, well!"—A third stands at the door—
" You, sir, your name, your business too;
   Tell me your woes, I ask no more."

" I married once; I married twice;
   Wife number two in peace departed;
What could a widower find to do?
   I was so *very* broken-hearted?"

" What! married thrice! You blessèd fool,"
   Replied the saint—" Twice I could pardon;
Twice rescued, cast yourself away?
   Be off! for not a single 'farden'

Of all Heaven's wealth is meant for those
   Who really know not how to use
The boons that on them are bestowed;
   Be off! you idiot, fool, and goose!"

AN OMNIUM-GATHERUM "PRICE LIST."

I was idle, and took up a book at a chance,
And soon I began through its pages to glance;
I found 'twas a " price list," well-thumbed and
   well-worn,

With its first and last pages all tattered and torn;
It came from our " Stores," its condition was shady,
And 'twas easy to see it belonged to a lady.

" Why, what's here?" I remarked, with a smile, to
    my wife.
" Rather ask, ' What's not here ? ' It's just so, on
    my life :
It's a modern Noah's ark—a remarkable hive—
But with most of the articles dead, not alive."

I turned over the pages again and again,
And a thousand odd notions passed quick through
    my brain :
Well, I'll look through this list of all possible things
That the care of a household to womankind brings.

There are " things " for the kitchen and " things "
    for the hall,
" Things " for bedrooms, for drawing-rooms, stables
    and all;
" Things " for store-room, for cabinet, pantry, and
    cupboard—
The reverse of what met the sad eyes of Dame
    Hubbard.

Well, we'll take a brief glance at our list of these
    " things ";
Here are dog-whips and telescopes, mirrors, gold
    rings,
Ladies' " knickers "—whatever those articles may
    be—
Teacups, parasols, hencoops, and dolls for the baby.

Pills, powders, and draughts, " puppy biscuits,"
    and purses,

Fruits preserved and **fruits potted,** and "aprons **for** nurses,"
Baby-linen, backgammon boards, poultices, muffs,
Carriage-baskets, calves' tongues, toilet-cans, powder-puffs;

With hand-basins, brass **fireguards, soft** easy **chairs,**
Blotting-books, paper-cases, **and** carpets for stairs,
Sheets, blankets, rugs, counterpanes, eiderdown quilts,
Greatcoats, pocket-handkerchiefs, crutches, and stilts;

Rifle guns, pocket-pistols (revolvers now styled),
Ales of "Bass" and of "Allsopp," both "bitter" and "mild,"
Four-in-hands, broughams, cabs, britskas, and all sorts of carriages,
And articles useful in prospect of marriages:

"Aunt Sallies" and cricket-stumps, bats, balls, and leggings,
"Things" for golf, for lawn-tennis and polo, tent-peggings,
Dump-bells, racquet-bats, quoits, rocking-horses and hobbies,
And "sword-helmets," *not* **such as are** issued to "bobbies."

Here are boxing-gloves, fencing-foils, sausages, soap,
Soups and gravies, all fit for the Queen or the Pope;
Memorandum books (ruled and unruled), jellies, jams,
Toothpicks, **warm** Witney blankets, Westphalian hams;

Books, sunshades, ear-trumpets and Japanese trays,

Slippers, garters, papouches, and fair ladies' stays,
" Dress-improvers," and " ladies' companions " by
    dozens,—
Pretty presents, I'm sure, for our dear country
    cousins.

Brazen fenders, fire-shovels, and pokers and tongs,
Pianos and harpsichords, dumb-bells and gongs;
Last, not least, though I fear you'll suspect me of
    scoffing,
(May it long be *not* wanted for use), is a coffin!

ELLICOTT SKINFLINT.

Old Ellicot Skinflint was " Cock of the Trade,"
For Ellicott Skinflint a fortune had made;
And his name and his credit stood high in " The
    Row,"
But the question is " stood they deservedly so ?"

Some men make a fortune by honest intentions
Carried honestly out; some by patent inventions;
Others rise by mere chance, no one knows how or
    cares,
And by fluke upon lucky fluke " tumble up stairs."
Others rise by the habit of storing small gains,
Others prosper by picking their poor neighbours'
    brains:
Others rise by schemes teeming with fraud, more
    or less,
Then, with eyes turn'd to heaven, will Providence
    bless.

Others spider-like sit in the midst of a web,
And watch for poor writers whose fortune's at ebb;

Smile, beckon, and bid them walk into their **snare,**
Then swallow them **up as a** wolf does **a** hare.

But Skinflint the simplest of patents had taken
For a far better thing than just " saving his bacon; "
Hard bargains he'd drive **with poor** authors. His thrift
Was simply to use them, then turn them adrift.

He would **suck out** their brains and would work them until
He had **made** them go round like **a** horse in **a** mill;
And **when they** cried out for the shadow of pay,
He'd reply, " **Go! be off;** or I'll send you away."

Yet he started **by** selling of leaflets **a pile,**
" Goody-goodies," and such like, and " tracts " by the mile;
And **the** tracts **and the** " **goodies** " alike they ran so—
" **Pray do always to** others **as you'd** be done *to.*"

Oh! **lesson too often** forgotten by **all,** Sirs,
By learned **and** simple, by great men and small, Sirs;
And I fear that **old** Skinflint, athirsting for gold,
Did not much **care** to swallow the medicines he sold.

No! Skinflint from rising to setting **of** sun, Sir,
Would **not** rest till he'd fairly (?) Jew'd each mother's son, Sir;
Cheeseparing and stingy and **mean** above any,
Ne'er, save by compulsion, **he'd** part with **a penny.**

Nay, he'd grudge his poor authors ink, **paper, and** quills,

And, he'd huckster with printers, and cut down
    their bills;
"Authors' proofs" and "corrections," and costs of
    that kind,
He would strike out as luxuries "not to his mind."

But 'twas not by thus acting the bully and strong
    man,
Prosper'd princely **John Murray** and worthy Tom
    Longman;
They were generous, and kindly, and honest all
    round,
And fair wages would pay for fair work, I'll be
    bound.

But thank God there must needs come a reckoning
    day,
When old Skinflint shall pass and be turned into
    clay;
Then the groans of poor printer's and poorer scribes'
    tears,
As he mounts up to heaven (?) shall ring in his ears.

"MONS. LE DUC."

Founded on Fact.

Belgravian matrons and maids, have a care!
Tyburnian mothers and widows, beware!
For "The Campbells are coming,"—I mean foreign
    swells—
How I wish they were off to their foreign "Hotels!"

And beware, inexperienced and fair "country
    cousins,"

For we've Barons, and **Viscounts, and** Counts, **too,**
    in dozens ;
And Marquises, too, not at all " rich " or " rare,"
Are cropping up thick in Park, Crescent, and Square.

Yes ! **and** e'en of **a** Duke, **too,** that very shy bird,
In Marylebone Gardens the note has been heard ;
And this " Duke " from afar, with his dignified airs,
Lives aloft **in a** garret up four pair of **stairs.**

Now **this** " Duke " is **a** great philosophical lion ;
He **has** written some books ; there's " The Trumpet
    of Zion,"
And of pseudo-prophetical pamphlets a score ;
Thy French rival, John Cumming, I own, is a bore.

But with ladies a dangerous thing is a man
Who styles himself " Duc **de** la Branc," or " De
    Span,"
And his shoulders shrugs up **in** a mystical way ;
But then most when he's reticent, learned, and gay.

It is true that his coronet may not be gold,
That his wealth (or his poverty) may be untold,
That his strawberry-leaves may prove tinsel and
    paste,
That his broad lands at best **are a** desolate waste.

But oh ! then **he's a** " Duke." **Only** think of the
    fame,
The *éclat* of that magic and grand-sounding name ;
For, as gingerbread gilt will an infant take in,
True or sham " Duke," the ladies care never a **pin.**

When **he** lounges about **in** the Park, at the " Zoo,"
How **the women** flock **round** him ! A dozen or two

You may see on a Fête day surrounding " His
   Grace ; "
Ah ! the " Zoo " is a terribly dangerous place.

How they listen whene'er the " Duke " opens his
   beak,
As though Jupiter Ammon or Phœbus would speak ;
Drink his words—not his wine. For a man worth
   a million
Port is all very well ; he sports only " Rousillon."

In the Anthropological line all he can
Is to show " Smith " at once may be monkey and
   man
And thus all unawares, by a fortunate fluke,
Proves a man may at once be an ape and a " Duke ! "

If Monsieur—I beg pardon—if ever " His Grace "
Deigns to prate of the Scytho-Cimmerian race,
While he stares when you quote from " The Father
   of History,"
To me such a *philosophe is* a great mystery.

When he talks of his Château in France near the
   seas,
And " the long waving line of the blue Pyrenees,"
Have a care ; for, in spite of your trouble and pain,
His estate may turn out *un chateau en Espagne !*

So, fair ladies, unless you 're ambitious of scandal,
Don't flutter like moths round this small ducal
   candle ;
Giddy butterflies, each one and all have a care ;
Susceptible maidens and widows, beware.

If they play the tame cat and will sit on your
   " soffy,"

Let them nibble your biscuits and sip tea and coffee;
But, though Humboldts in Ante-Mosaic cosmogony,
Never put their feet under your fathers' mahogany.

Yes, in town, like some mushroom or fungussy thing,
Foreign "Dukes" crop up thick with the rain of
    the spring,
And when not quite unquestioned their title and
    right,
They fly off, like blind owls, under shelter of night.

So, be warned, giddy moths, of "Counts," "Barons,"
    and "Dukes;"
Rash ventures in Cupid's domain are but "flukes."
All they want is your money, which when they
    have ta'en,
Bless your stars if you e'er see a stiver again.

HORACE PARAPHRASED.

SEE BOOK, II. ODE IV.

What, down in the dumps, man? Come, cheer up,
    my hearty!
  Farewell to all sorrow, and drive away care!
Though smit with the charms of a servile young
    party,
  There's no need to blush up to the roots of your
    hair.

Why, Achilles the brave, and the great Alexander,
  To Briseis and Thais their freedom resigned;
And kings, heroes, and many a gallant commander,
  Have bowed down to slaveys for time out of mind.

The fair Emma* she quitted her dust-pan and brushes
  To vanquish the victor of great Trafalgar,
Whom she brought to her feet as a suppliant suitor;
  Thus proving that "peace has it conquests," like war.

Even Wellington, he whom no perils could soften,
  From his battles and sieges when safe in his tent,
Reposed 'neath his laurels *non solus*, and often
  Cheered his heart with the smiles of a fair maid from Kent.

Then stand to your guns, man, and stick to your Helen,
  Such a girl was ne'er bred by a villain or churl;
Talk of nobles and gentles! In sooth, there's no telling
  She's the far from unnatural child of an earl.

Why, she sings like a lark of the deeds of her clansmen
  While sweeping your staircase and lighting your fires;
And I'm told Sally vows, though I never have heard her,
  She can boast of broad acres once owned by her sires.

Then blush not to own the impeachment so tender;
  In your Helen seek comfort, seek solace, and joy.
Though she's fair, young, and frolicsome, trust me she never
  Will cost you one teardrop, or fire a new Troy.

---

*Emma Lyon, a nursemaid, and afterwards a housemaid, lived to become Lady Hamilton, and to help Nelson in gaining one of his victories.

Her sweet face, her bright eyes, and her tapering
    ankles
Might well stir the heart of an amorous youth;
And her bosom so tenderly swelling might tempt
    him—
But I, my dear friend, am just sixty; that's truth.

A DISTANT DAY! A PROPHECY.

Yes! when the sun shall cease to shine,
    The moon to shed her ray,
When Sol's bright beams shall rule the night,
    And stars shall gild the day:

When streams flow upward to the hills,
    When front shall turn to rear,
When wives from curtain-lectures cease,
    And hounds from chasing dear;

When sharks shall toddle down the Strand,
    And Dukes give place to Earls;
When soldiers shall from glory shrink,
    Nor women care for pearls;

When men no longer tipple ale,
    And age gives place to youth;
(Oh! wonder of all wonders), then
    Liars shall—speak the truth!

CHRISTMAS; AN ACROSTIC.
(From "*Once a Week*.")

O! there are joys that hoar December brings,
Nor flaunting Summer knoweth; children's eyes

Can shed glad brightness o'er the moodiest hearth.
E'en sorrow **dries** her tears when childhood smiles
And gives the rein of joy. Yet some there be
Who wrap themselves in sad and blank despair,
Ever forgetful of the voice that spake
"Earth, be at peace! welcome good will to men!
"Kind hearts can make this world a Paradise!"

TO MISS ———

Mary, forgive a serious word:
   When once **you** see **your friend**'s repenting,
Say, is it noble, is it wise,
   To be so very unrelenting?

I wrong'd you, but I meant no wrong;
   I harm'd you, **but I** meant no harm;
Write, speak; **restore** my banished peace,
   And bid **this** storm give place **to** calm.

I've learnt a lesson, nor will tax
   Friendship too far again, I vow:
Oh! if forgiveness be fit work
   For angels, be **an** angel now.

RECIPE FOR A NOVEL AFTER G. P. R. JAMES.

Take a cliff by the sea with the sun's parting ray,
Two travellers each leading his horse by a bay,
Two dark-visaged gipsies, a rich woodland scene,
Some villagers keeping their feast on a green;
A church and a castle,—in ruins of course,—

A social sin follow'd by fits of remorse;
A " Girl of the period," a nice morning call,
A dinner at Willis's rooms, and a ball;
A self-will'd young " swell," an intriguing mamma,
A run-away match, and the wrath of papa:
These materials provided, the ends made to meet,
Write away—and you'll find that your novel's
    complete,
" In three volumes post, Colburn, Marlborough
    Street."

TO E. M. P.

Dear cousin, though in various ways,
    We're both inclined to wrong;
With *me* the flesh, I own, is weak;
    With *you* the Spirit's strong.

Then henceforth sworn between us be
    This compact firm and true,—
You, Emma, shall look after me,
    And I'll look after you.

Thus through this vale of smiles and tears,
    True sister and true brother,
Or " Cook-and-footman-like,—"see Boz—*
    We'll each improve the other.

---

*The reference is to Nicholas Nickleby, Chapt. XVI. "**Three**
"serious footmen: cook, housemaid, and nursemaid; each female
"servant required to join the Little Bethel Congregation three
"times every Sunday, with a serious footman. If the cook is
"more serious than the footman, she will be expected to improve
"the footman; and if the footman is more serious than the cook,
"he will be expected to improve the cook."

A VALENTINE.

Addressed by me in 1868 to my cousin, Miss Emma M. Pearson, along with a Shetland Shawl. Miss Pearson, two years later, on my recommendation, was sent out to the seat of war, under the auspices of the Red Cross Society (founded mainly by members of the English Langue of our Order of St. John) to superintend the nursing of the sick and wounded. Her chief scene of labours after Sedan, at which she was present, was Orleans, where she was most highly esteemed by Bishop Dupanloup. The remainder of her life was devoted to works of charity, and she died at Florence, much regretted and lamented, in the summer of 1893.—R.I.P.

Forgive me if, though far away,
   Dear cousin Emma, cousin mine,
I send you this fine frosty morn,
   A trifling little Valentine.

It's cosy, light, and soft to touch,
   And though on Zetland's shores 'twas spun,
It's warm and cool at once, and will
   Shield your fair neck from wind and sun.

You'll find it no bad thing when birds
   Mate in the woods this very day:
Not bad in storms of blustering March,
   'Mid April showers or winds of May.

Take it and bind it round your neck,
   And lay its ends upon your breast.
What need of long and ample folds?
   Your warm heart needs no lengthened vest.

Yes, to all friends and strangers warm,
   Loving, unselfish, fond and true,
For others' griefs that heart has bled,
   Far more than others bled for you.

Well! cherish others if you will,

Just like this little Shetland tie;
But, Emma, don't forget, " at home
   Begins the work of charity."

Think of yourself, your gallant self;
   Be wise in time; be wise to-day:
Spite of the glorious Sun o'erhead
   Cold winds blow oft in treacherous May.

Reckless of future cost, you joy
   In your Spring time of health and beauty;
But think, when Summer's past away
   Care for yourself may prove a duty.

But to be careless of your health
   Sure, sister, friends, will never let you:
And more—though you forget yourself,
   There's one at least will ne'er forget you!

ANOTHER VALENTINE.

Addressed more than twenty years ago to a lady since dead.

It is St. Valens' Eve, the night
   That ushers in St. Valens' day;
So, fool-like, I resolve to write,
And a brief Valentine indite,
   Altho' I scarce know what to say,

Nor yet to whom.   Yet, stay, I know
   One lady free from spleen and malice,
Brave, constant, generous, noble too,
And more than passing fair to view,
   Peerless in goodness, Madame Challis.

But what to say? I cannot prate
  Of Cupids small with painted wings,
Each grinning at his stupid mate;
Doves, churches, bowers, are out of date,
  And all those thrice-familar things

Sold in small shops. Yet friends, I trow,
  And friendships are not bought and sold:
Then let me tell her, though she know it,—
The word is that of more than poet.—
  True friends are worth their weight in gold.

She kindly deigns to call me friend:
  God grant that I may prove a true one;
And if I fail,—which Heaven forfend—
To fill my place, then, so I end,
  God grant that she may find a new one!

"ALL MEN ARE LIARS." (Psalm cxvi., 10).

" In my great haste " (the words are wide),
" All men are liars," David cried;
  Such was his royal pleasure:
But had he lived in London now,
At its west end, he might, I vow,
  Have said it " at his leisure."
And if in these deceitful days,
When woman sets the town ablaze
  With foul malignant tongue,
David had said " some women too
Are liars," why, 'twixt me and you,
  The King had not been wrong.

A HOMELY PARODY.

> "Little drops of water,
>   Little grains of sand,
> Make the mighty ocean
>   And the beauteous land."
> —*Village School Song.*

Little drops of water
  Pour'd into the milk,
Make the milkman's daughter
  Dress in beauteous silk.

Little fibs so trifling
  Told at neighbour's table,
Make black lies and gratify
  The "gentleman in sable."

ON RECEIVING A PRESENT OF GAME.

Of pheasants and hares and such like pleasant things
  You are daily augmenting my store :
But were I to say half what I feel, I should seem
  Like an "Oliver asking for more."

TO JANE, WITH A VIOLET.

Dear Jane, forgive—I know you'll not forget—
The sender of this Attic violet,
  Who cries *peccavi* with his heart's regret.

AT CHRISTMAS-TIDE; BY A CYNIC.

What mean these boughs of mistletoe and holly ?
Small boys, I own, may vote them "awful jolly" ?
To me they seem the very height of folly,
                    At Christmas-tide.

Of beef and turkey Maud has eat her fill;
Mince-pies have made our Edward very ill;
And I, their luckless sire, must pay the bill
     At Christmas-tide.

Next will come Christmas boxes—butchers' boys,
Sweeps, postmen, scavengers, with ceaseless noise,
Enough to sicken one of all such joys,
     At Christmas-tide.

Yet stay: I know a trick worth two of that;
I'll dine next year within my tiny flat,
And hobnob with my parrot, dog, and cat,
     At Christmas-tide.

TO CLARA ——

Oh! Lady Clare, oh! Lady Clare,
 In vain your sermon pen you ply;
The monkey o'er your husband's arms
 Cares for such lectures more than I.

TRUTH *v.* LIES.

If I rightly remember, I learnt in my youth,
That God is the God of love, mercy aud *truth;*
But in these later days to my utter surprise
It seems He's put forth as the lover of "lies,"
Or at least their approver; but how can that be,
I own, is a puzzle "betwixt you and me."

TO MY ALMA MATER.

" How comes it, Oxford, thou dost bear the fame

"Of one grand store-house of all useful knowledge?"
"My son, I know not, save that all men say
"Each freshman brings some tiny store my way,
  "But carries little back again from college."

THE DECADE DECAYED.

When the Décade met lately in Silvester's rooms
  The "Scout" a sad blunder he made;
"They have done with the wine, Bob; but ere they goes off
  Ten coffees they want—the Decáde."

O sad slip of that "member unruly," the tongue,
  O blunder of terrible power:
The "Décade" that night met its first fatal wound,
  It came the "Decáyed" from that hour.

"*Vox nescit reverti emissa,*" alas!
  We know from old Horace's page;
Sad and short then the life of that scholarly club
  Destined never to reach its old age.

From ten members it dwindled to nine, then to eight,
  Then to seven, then to six, then to five;
But when the survivors to four were reduced
  It was rather more dead than alive.

Then it died, and a memory dear of its past
  Is all that remains in its room:
"*Requiescat in pace*" all Oxford will write
  Shedding tears of regret on its tomb.

L

DR. WATTS' LIBEL ON DOGS.

*Some **well-known** Lines Paraphrased.*

Dogs *don't* "delight to bark and bite"
   'Xcept butchers set them to :
"Lions and bears" *don't* "growl and fight;"
   They've something else to do.

But Christians of the self same fold
   Bid their vile passions rise,
And school their tongues, if not their "hands,"
   To "tear each other's eyes."

A "TIMES" ADVERTISEMENT AND ITS ANSWER.

In the *Times* of April 4th, 1872, appeared the following poetical advertisement :—

Required by a gent, near to Bromley, in Kent,
A cook, on plain cooking sincerely intent.
She need not make *entremets*, sauces or jellies,
That cause indigestion and irritate bellies ;
Enough if she's able to serve up a dinner
That won't make her master a dyspeptic grinner.
If asked to make bread, no excuse she must utter ;
Must be able to churn and to make melted butter.
If these she can do, and eke boil a potato,
And cook well a chop with a sauce called tomato,
The writer won't care to apply further test
That she's up to her work, and knows all the rest.
Be she honest, industrious, sober, and clean,
And neat in her garb, not a highly-dress'd quean ;
And she must be content, whatever her age is,
With sugar and tea, and £20 wages.
—Address, W. G. E., Post Office, Bromley, Kent.

To the above I sent an answer on the same day, in

the following terms on behalf of a servant who was about
to leave me, and who, I should add, got the situation.

Sir, I've seen your "advert;" can, I think, meet
    your wishes;
Can cook a plain dinner of joints and made dishes;
Am just twenty-three, and, though not plain in looks,
Am equal to many who rank as *plain* cooks.
My character closest inspection won't fear, sir;
And—further particulars I'm anxious to hear, sir.

"MY PIANO AND I"; A DIALOGUE.

"So madame wants my instrument,"
    Says I to Mary Anna;
Well, then, as tables turn, I'll try
    And question my "pianner."

"Good tuneful friend, come, tell me true,
    Say, will you quit my parlour,
And go and live in Surrey there,
    With 'Fluffy,' 'Poll,' and 'Snarler?'"

"No! You're a master good and kind,
    And always were, d'ye see, Sir;
And though I've lived with you ten years,
    You ne'er laid hands on me, Sir.

"But madame E—— will work me hard,
    And thump, and strum, and beat me;
So, master dear, I'll cling to you,
    And chance it how you treat me.

"Your rooms are small, but still I hope,
    I ain't much in your way, Sir;
And when the ladies come to tea,
    How sweet on me they play, Sir.

"I'm only a 'pianner,' but
   I has my tender feeling;
I'm sure to weep if sent away,
   Past memories o'er me stealing—

"I'm only a 'pianner,' but
   If this last word I utter,
Kind Sir, I knows full well, I does,
   Vich side my bread is butter.

"What! me desire a change? No fear!
   So tell your Mary Anna,
Where master is not welcome quite,
   There won't go his 'pianner!'"

EPIGRAMS.

ON H.H. POPE LEO XIII.

These lines, being forwarded with a version in Latin to His Holiness at Rome, were rewarded by the sending of Pope Leo's special blessing to the writer.

To guard his fold from lions is the worldly
      shepherd's art;
But in the Church the Lion plays the faithful
      Shepherd's part.

IN MEMORIAM H.E. CARDINAL MANNING.
JAN. 14, 1892.

(Translated from the original Latin by the same author).

Prince of the Church and Cardinal! we mourn
Thy loss, our loss. All England mourns thee dead;
Its princes and its nobles weep. For thou

Living didst earn thy name, "The poor man's
        friend:"
And long that name shall live. Worn out with age,
From life-long labours freed, thou did'st lay down
The burden of thy being. Ever thou
Did'st for the toilers toil; their rights thine own
Thou did'st account, and sparing of thy self
Wert thine own conqueror; say, can greater praise
To man accrue? Yea! thou did'st pass from life
Contented, pilgrim-wise; for nought to thee
Were wealth and grandeur. Hence it comes that
        thou
Art called the Sire and brother of the poor.

ON AN ECCENTRIC OLD GENTLEMAN.

A lawyer's sharp letter, I fear nothing less,
  Will wake up Mr. Gilbert's attention;
Well, well! I'm afraid that his Marylebone den
  Is a terrible "House of Detention;"
He keeps there his old bags, his old boots, his old
    shoes,
  And also the books of his brother,
Who so kind and so thoughtful once lent them, but
    now
  Will be blest if he lends him another.

TO AN ATTORNEY WHO OFFERED ME ADVICE GRATIS.

Oh! Barker, oh! Barker, it was not "quite nice"
At the chapel-door steps to give gratis advice;
And I own that I think it the mark of a "cad" man,
In the presence of children to lecture a "dad," man.

E'en a barrister's nothing apart from a fee,
And a lowbred attorney is not a "Q.C."
But belongs to a class at "the foot of the hill"
In whose "depths" there are "deeps" that sink
    "lower" down still.
Should I e'er need your counsel and want you to
    prate, sir,
I can call at your office and leave "six and eight,"
    sir.

AT THE "ODD VOLUMES."

"These old playing cards," said our good brother
    Clulow,
"Were wholly unknown to the primitive Zulu,
  "And never were seen in Rome, Athens, or Veii;"
But dear brother Liley, he whispered so slyly,
  "Yet I've seen those same pips on the walls of
    Pompeii."

THE PROFIT OF BEING LATE.

For shooting an innocent lad with a pistol,
Tom was left to be hung at the 'Sizes at Bristol.
Jack Ketch "would be sharp at the jail-door at
    eight;"
He'd "another job elsewhere, and that would not
    wait."
Tom came leisurely down at a quarter to nine,
And found himself late for the hangman's long
    twine;
Then to breakfast sat down like a person of
    "quality,"
Having saved his own neck by his unpunctuality.

A THREE-BOTTLE MAN.

Those two bottles of sherry ! why ? where are they
 gone ?
 I'm afraid you've drank more than you ought,
  dear :
" You *must* have had help." "Yes, indeed, that I
  had ;
 I'd the help of—a bottle of port, dear ! "

A BEE IN HIS BONNET.

A Scotchman when queer,—take my word, man,
 upon it,—
Is said to have sometimes " a bee in his bonnet ; "
But worse the condition of poor brother Ned,
He's got bee, wasp, and hornet at once in his head.

IMPROMPTU.

To a bride on carrying off from a party the hat of her husband.

I unwittingly " collared " your husband's silk hat,
And most penitent ask your forgiveness for that :
Yet the sin was but small ; for what *would* you
 have said,
If in lieu of his hat I had " collared " his head ?
And, dear lady, think how I'd have made you to
 start,
If in place of his *head* I had borne off his *heart !*

SISTERS: WITH A DIFFERENCE.

Tom's daughters are unlike ; indeed, I fear,
One's for *mere cash*, the other for *Cashmere*.

ON THE WALFORD ARMS AND CREST.

Our arms, by all heraldic rules,
Are a fierce lion *passant gules*:
Our crest a lion, far from tame,
Bears a *cross-crosslet of the same*.
For three long centuries, I note,
" *Fortis et stabilis* " we wrote
For motto: I, who've learnt what are
Life's struggles, write " *Per Ardua.*"
But one wit of our family
Adds a new motto, cunningly
Suggesting " *Fortis* [est] *ut Leo
Cui fides* [certa stat] *in Deo.*

COMPOSED NEAR SNOWDON.

Come now, old grumbler! don't complain;
  Old Snowdon's wet, 't is true;
Why not? like most, he daily takes
  A drop of " mountain dew."

MARRIAGE; A REPLY.

" What? Marry *la belle veuve?* I've no such intention;
  I assure you, dear Charles, as I value my life;
Au contraire I've ten reasons *sans* any invention,
  For she has nine children, and I have—a wife."

A PURITAN DEFINED.

Pray tell me what 's a Puritan?
A sanctimonious sort of man,
  Who mixes " Sabbath " up with " Sunday ";
Who rules by terror of the rod,
And substitutes for love of God
  The fear of awful Mrs. Grundy.

CHRISTMAS FOOLS.

Christmas comes with lots of folly,
Mistletoe green and berried holly.
Now what's the meaning?—" Green are they
" Who look for pleasure on this day;
" And those who dream to banish care,
" Blush red to think what fools they are!"

THE DYING POACHER.

"John Hodge," says the Vicar, "and now that you're dying,
 Forgive the old squire; yes, your duty is plain."
With a pause, replies Hodge, "If I dies I'll forgive 'un;
 But if I gets well, I'll be at 'un again."

ON A ROBBER SWINGING ON A GIBBET.

"What is this that I see? cries the innocent Kate,
 "What? a gibbet, and on it a robber! how cruel!"
"Don't be shock'd now, for since Tom was lifted aloft
"There's one rogue less on earth; so be asy, my jewel."

SHAM STRAWBERRY LEAVES.
A Fact.

As I was walking down the Strand one day,
 A horse—I pledge you, sir, my word upon it,—
Put forth his mouth as though to eat some hay,
 And snatched a wheat-ear off a lady's bonnet.
Just so, me thought, and just by such a fluke,
 A wanton widow whom gay love deceives,
Essayed one day to catch a pseudo-duke,
 And munched a mouthful of sham strawberry leaves.

THE FIFTH COMMANDMENT; NEW VERSION.

"Honour my child" ('twas written once)
 "Thy father and thy mother too."

"Honour thy daughter and thy son"—
  That's how *we* read the precept new.

Yes; in this fast-progressing age
  We really scarce know what we read;
And, e'er another decade's flown,
  "Honour thy grandson" may succeed.

REMONSTRANCE ON A THREATENED CLEARANCE TO MAKE A RAILWAY STATION.

So they're going to "clear" twenty streets and a
    square!
But what Goths those "improvers" of neighbour-
    hoods are!
  What *can* for destruction atone?
Why, only to mention the scheme is repellent;
Solitudinem faciunt, "*Station*" *appellant**;—
  Pray "let it severely alone."

"LEGGE v. YATES"; A LIBEL CASE.

These Libel suits may, as a rule
  Attest the man of mettle;
But this strange cause, "Legge v. Yates,"
  Means simply "pot and kettle."

ON CHAS. BRADLAUGH, M.P.

From a Tory point of view.

Why does Northampton's town return Charles
    Bradlaugh?
Because Northampton town is under Cad-Law.

**Solitudinem faciunt, pacem appellant.—Tacit.*

LAND AND WATER.

When Columbus first sighted America's strand,
Overjoyed at the view, he cried " Land ! comrades,
    Land !
But our doctor on tapping his patient, Bob Porter,
In the joy of his heart cried " why, Water ! here's
    Water."

TO MRS.——ON THE DEATH OF HER FOX TERRIER.

So Nelly's dead and gone ! alas !
  Yet, think, to make amends,
Kind Providence has left you still
  A tongue to bite your friends.

ON MY DOG CARLO.

My dog's a sad Tory ; deny it who can ;
For he strongly objects to the plain " working man ;"
If a working man calls, Carlo's apt to show fight,
And instead of a *vote* he will give him a *bite*.

BESANT THE EDITOR.

Proudly Besant upriseth, and sniffeth the air with
    his nostrils :
  " I am an Editor grand ; not a mere slavey am I.
Dare ye disturb my repose? I've a beautiful view
    of the mountains
  Down in the valley of Wales. Printer and
    author be—blest."

ON STOCK, THE PUBLISHER.

When in Dec. 1880 I ceased to edit the Antiquary, (which I founded), the Athenæum announced that the Magazine in future would be edited by two F.S.A's.

If he who aids the patient ass
By multiplying blades of grass
   Doth much increase our store,
What thanks to Stock should authors give,
Who bids *two* Editors to live
   Where *one* has starved before!

AUTHORS AND PUBLISHERS.

"That jurymen may live, let wretches hang,"
Wrote Pope. Away with all such stupid slang!
Henceforth,—thank Stock,—read we the latter line,
"Let authors starve that publishers may dine"!

FUR PRÆDESTINATUS.

"As if the necessity which is supposed to destroy the injustice of murder, for instance, would not also destroy the injustice of punishing it.—*Butler's Analogy, part* 1, *chapter* 6.

"I stole, 'tis true; but yet my hand was driven
By stern necessity forced on from Heaven."
"Well sir, you were compelled to steal. If true,
So likewise *I'm compelled to punish you*.

A DEODAND.

Twixt "Deodand" and "Deodate"
   Conflicting were opinions;

Some thought both words the same—as like
  As "inions" are to "inions."
Uprose the scholar straight and spake,
  "The differences, I'll state 'em ;—
A tithe is *'Deo Dandum'* : *'Nil'*
  Too oft is *'Deo Datum.'*"

JEDBURGH JUSTICE.

What? talk of "Justice"? "Courts of Law"?
"Judges" and "Juries"? Hold your jaw!
  Such things are only fit for laughter:
In this our little border town,
By old tradition handed down,
  We hang men first and try them after.

LIFE AND DEATH.

Ask what is life? On questions such as this
God and the world for ever are at strife.
"Life," says the world, "is but the path to death;"
"Death," says the saint, "is but the path to life."

THE VEGETARIAN SPEAKS.

Time was when mankind lived on nothing but roots
And green innocent herbs and all primitive fruits;
But when fig-leaves the fashion became, in that day
Man took to eat flesh in an impious way,*
And from that time to this we are quite in the dark
"Whether Shark eat you, Massa, or Massa eat
    Shark."

---

*Ante Impia quam cæsis gens est epulata juvencis.—Virg. Georg. ii., 537.

Yes! since then man lives chiefly on mutton and veal,
Or on chicken and beef makes unthinking a meal;
But oh! *could* we go back to the prime of Dame Nature,
And dine but once more on a turnip or 'tatur,
Our innocent souls in our innocent skins
Would be free from all fevers, and sickness, and sins;
And when life and its scenes and its joys fade away,
We should pass into Heav'n by kind Nature's decay.

DARWIN *v.* MOSES.

In the days of our childhood, dear sir and dear madam,
We believed all about mother Eve and *père* Adam;
But Darwin has taught us that Moses is wrong,
That creation itself 's a mere myth, a mere song;
That, like Topsy, we grew, or a sponge, or a 'tatur,
And owed not existence to any Creator.
If such be the case, it strikes *me*, the solution
Of our earthly existence is mere " evolution ";
Little monkeys the dads of humanity are, sir,
And a ring-tail'd baboon was our primitive pa', sir.

"PROPRIUM EST ODISSE QUEM LAESERIS."

'Tis nothing strange that Mr. Smith
   Should hate me; for, you see
It is not that *I've* injured *him*,
   But that *he's* injured *me*.

"SIRS, YE ARE BRETHREN"!

Since all are parts of one great whole,

And man to man is brother;
True t'is that one good turn deserves
But rarely gets—another.

DIVIDE ET IMPERA.

Learn, boy, to add and to subject,
And then proceed to multiply,
Next to divide—and you will rule
A village teacher by and by.

ON AN ILL-APPOINTED MARRIAGE.

"Well Jack, and how is Mrs. Captain B.?
She and her husband are ill-matched, I'm told."
"Not so; the bargain struck between them's fair;
She has been bought, I vow, and he's been sold."

EVE AND THE SERPENT.

Our first father, they say, brought us sin;
I rather ascribe it to Madam;
Though the snake tempted grandmother Eve,
Yet t'was Eve tempted grandfather Adam.

ON LORD SACKVILLE'S CLOSING KNOWLE PARK, KENT, TO THE PUBLIC IN 1883.

If England's Peers were all so many Sack-villes,
Then England's Peers would soon be turned to
    lack-villes.
No need of Dilkes and Laboucheres and Rads, Sir,
The Lords would perish by their foolish "fads," Sir.

ON A RECENT ELECTION AT GUILDHALL.

" Vote for Sir Crœsus ! he's so rich " !—
" Wealth is to me no commendation :
" Wiser by far, I'll vote for those
" Who've lost, not gain'd, by speculation."

THORLEY'S CATTLE-FOOD.

Jim writes from Wadham, and he sends me this,
   The latest bit of Oxford tittle-tattle :—
" Thorley 's made tutor. What say *you*, my friend"?
   " Why ? that his lectures will be 'food for cattle.' "

SERVANTS' EXCUSES.

"Oh ! Sir," says Mary Jane to me,
   " That scratch upon the dining table
Was made before I came to you ;
   Upon my word, good Sir, 'tis true ;
   To swear it I am really able."

Yes ; so, just so, in Eden's bower
   Adam and Eve in earth's first prime
Made like complaint, and answer got
From Echo—(servant girls were not)—
   " 'Twas done in t' other people's time."

ON A LADY WHO SENT LILIES TO OUR CHURCH FOR A HARVEST FESTIVAL.

Shine white, fair lilies, in our minster's gloom !
Shine while ye live, here shed your latest bloom !

A living lily is a precious prize ;
Lilies with heads cut off are simply—lies.

A SUIT FOR "RESTITUTION OF CONJUGAL RIGHTS."

" What ! force an unwilling spouse back to your
    arms ?
  You'd do better, dear H——, if you list to my
    song ;
" Why ? the forced restitution of conjugal rights
  Is the perpetuation of conjugal wrong."

COLLISIONS.

" Why the '*Druid*' run down the smack '*Nile*,'
    dear, is tried
  In the Probate, Divorce, and Heaven knows
    what Division."
" Yes, as wives with their husbands, like ships, will
    ' collide,'
  One court settles domestic and naval collision."

ON A CERTAIN PUBLISHER.

Does your boy want to learn all the " tricks of the
    trade " ?
Only send him to S—— and his fortune is made ! *

---

   *These lines were sent by me in reply to the following advertisement in the *Times*, Jan. 27th, 1885 :—" To Publishers.— " Wanted, to place a Youth, aged 16 years, with a good firm of " publishers, where he will get a thorough knowledge of the " business. Particulars to Mr.——, —— house, Hampstead, " N.W."

A GOOD INVESTMENT.

Most persons buy what most they need : so Ruth
Laid all her savings by and purchased—*Truth*.

A THOUGHT ON DEATH.

Fair lilies bloom in May, then straightway fade ;
   And roses fall soon as they pass their June :
No sooner smiles the primrose then 't is past ;
   But, Death, thou claim'st all seasons for thine
      own.

Part III.

LAYS OF VENTNOR.

PRELIMINARY LINES.

A Parody from Wordsworth.

Dance, dance! for here in Ventnor town
Beneath the breezy Bonchurch Down,
Dwells an old man who, though he bears
The weight of more than seventy years,
Lives in the light of youthful glee,
And he will dance and sing with thee.

"LONELY"?
A LAY IN PRAISE OF VENTNOR.

"What! lonely? You selfish ungrateful old man!
   Though you've got a sweet home by the side of
       the sea;
And a garden, and fowls, a pet dog, and a cat,
   And a store of good books? Why, pray what
       would you be"?

Oh! yes, I've a house with a garden behind,
   And green myrtles a-blooming in view of the sea,
And the kindest of nurses to wait on my wants;
   Yet friends think me as lonely as lonely can be.

Yes! I've known what it was to have business galore

To fill up every hour from breakfast to tea,
   To have clients in waiting to help and advise,
     And long letters to pen, authors, artists to see.*

But an end came to this, and "*emeritus*" quite
     From all such pleasant labours I found myself free,
And dull dreary "home duties" (so called) took their place,
     And my life *was* as weary as weary could be.

So I settled down here with the Downs in my rear,
     And with windows commanding a view of the sea
Ever changing and changing, yet ever the same;
     Pray, what fog-throttled Londoner envies not me?

Why, I cannot be lonely, asleep or awake,
     While in bodily health I'm as sound as can be,
Along with my dinner drink whisky or port,
     And at bed-time a mixture of G.R.O.G.

While I go to bed early, arise sharp at eight,
     And swallow at breakfast my coffee or tea,
Then go forth to my labours, my pleasures, my walks,
     Talk of dreariness, loneliness! Fiddle-de-Dee!

I take life as I find it: if, pestered with lies
     From the lips of false friends, why, what is it to me?
Women's tongues may wag on, Ananias† may fib,
     And Sapphira tell lies "by the side of the sea";

---

*For nearly ten years I was sub-Editor and afterwards Editor of "*Once a Week*," on which Millais, Tenniel, Leech, Walker, Lawless, Charles Keene, and other well-known artists (now nearly all dead) were employed.

†See Acts of the Apostles, v., 1—10.

But a lie is a lie if you leave it alone
  As sure as Old England's "the land of the free";
And the air of our Downs will blow falsehoods away,
  Yes! in beautiful Ventnor beside the blue sea.

Then if health and good spirits remain to me still,
  And if, having such joys, yet for others I pine,
All I say or can say 's "I'm a thankless old cuss,
  Should one feeling of loneliness ever be mine."

"A SOFT ANSWER."

An Epistle addressed to a young lady in Ventnor, who had given the author a fox-terrier puppy.

" A soft answer will turn away wrath,"
  Men say—so let's try if it will;
If it does not, the fault is not mine,
  But that of my ink or my quill.

I did *not* undervalue your gift:
  'Twas the dearest of puppies, I'm sure;
But I am not a trainer of dogs,
  And I do not live out on a moor;

I've no stables or yard with warm hay,
  And the nights are uncommonly frigid;
Had I left the poor fellow outside,
  By morn he'd been stark dead and rigid.

I felt you'd be grieved and annoyed,
  But I thought you'd have mastered your dander;
For who writes savage notes without cause
  To a "friend"—is a goose or a gander.

Father Drew, he has told us of late

"We should always be helpful and kind";
And I thought that a pious young lass
　Would have borne such a lesson in mind.

By this time you doubtless have learnt,
　What I thought in my letter I'd said,
I did *not* give your puppy away;
　But arranged just to "get him a bed,"

Till your wishes or rather commands
　In the matter could notified be,
Of course is a "sweet pretty note"
　From your house by "the side of the sea."

For the feelings of servants, I own,
　I have always a tender regard,
And in their attachment to me
　I reap a most ample reward.

I also try hard to consult
　The feelings of "friends" where I can,
And the feelings of pups in the frost,
　Nor my tenderness limit to man.

Your reproof and rebuke I accept;
　You are twenty and I'm sixty-nine;
But "It's never too late to amend";
　Then why should an old man repine,

Or give way to one feeling of wrath,
　If he learns a new lesson of duty
About puppies, and presents, and gifts,
　In life's eve from the lips of a beauty?

I intended no slight; and these lines
　For all slights, sure, should make full amends;
So let us shake hands, nor forget
　That "At Christmas we all should be friends."

"GOOD LORD, DELIVER ME"!

While Thee I serve or strive to serve,
   According to thy word,
From sorrow, sickness, grief and pain,
   Deliver me, Good Lord!

From riches, that will lead astray,
   My truant heart from Thee,
From discontent, from worldly cares,
   From grinding poverty;

Deliver me from secret snares
   Laid by mine enemies;
Deliver me from sudden death;
   Deliver me from—lies.

But chiefly while I dwell among
   The busy haunts of men,
Save me from Mrs. Gossip's tongue
   And Mrs. Smalltalk's pen.

THE BATTLE OF THE FLOWERS.

(I.)

How doth the busy Burna-Bee†
   Improve the shining hours,
And gather funds to help along
   The " Battle of the Flowers."

How skilfully he writes his notes,
   And seals with sealing-wax!
Nor toils to advertise one half
   The trouble that he takes!

In helping on this pleasant cause
   I would be busy too;

---

†The Rev. E. Burnaby.

> But really it is very hard
>   To know just what to do.
>
> Shine, sun! and our Committee men
>   Th' accounts will soon have passed,
> And we shall see in £. s. d.
>   A good result at last.

(II.)

In our recent "Battle," a stone, wrapped round with primroses, was thrown by a mischievous boy at a lady in one of the carriages, who put up her hand to protect her face, which otherwise might have been seriously injured. In the following lines I have endeavoured to draw a moral from the occurrence.

> It went off well; yet, by the powers,
> In our sweet "Battle of Flowers,"
>   One lady got a wound, sir.
> Struck by a primrose-coated stone
> From a boy's hand in mischief thrown,
>   She fainted not nor swoon'd, sir.
>
> The imp, asham'd at what he'd done,
> At once resolv'd to "cut and run,"
>   Nor stopped to beg for pardon:
> What pain he caused that lady fair—
> (Such wicked boys in Ventnor are)—
>   He "did'nt care a farden."
>
> The lady's wound soon healed, and she
> Forgave the boy; and so should we,
>   Struck not with stones but lies;
> Lies they will only graze the skin;
> If we can but forgive the sin,
>   They're "blessings in disguise."
>
> Yes! if our hearts be good and true,
> Pray we for those who cause us rue,

And cry " God's will be done ! "
Lies, they may rankle for a space,
But those who suffer win the race
Before the set of sun.

THE DONKEY'S COMPLAINT.

"TROUGH AND BUCKET"; A WORD FOR THE DONKEYS.

Pity the sorrows of a poor old " moke,"
   Whose trembling limbs have borne him to your door ;
Don't let your charity pass off in smoke ;
   Oh ! give relief, and heaven will bless your store.

" Bucket or trough " : it really matters nought
   So that relief be given ; for think, right soon
Spring will be past, and we in heat and drought
   Shall stand beneath the mid-day suns of June.

You fear " excess " on the moke's part ; you think
   We four-legged brutes shall more than take our fill ;
Such fears were better spent on men who drink
   All day in " pubs " upon the neighbouring hill !

As for the horse, he too is " up to snuff " ;
   From drinking-troughs you fear he'll catch the glanders !
Do dogs at shop-doors catch distemper ? Stuff !
   Away ! away ! with all such silly slanders !

" Bucket or trough " ? we cry, and still will cry ;
   Man, horse, dog, donkey, each to each his brother;
So kindly stir yourselves, Town Council, try !
   But give us quickly either one or other !

April, 1894.

THE TRIUMPH OF THE DONKEYS.

Sound the loud timbrel o'er Ventnor's blue sea ;
The donkeys have triumphed, the mokes they are free !
They are free, they are free ! they shall drink of the rill
That bubbles and leaps down the side of our hill !

No " bucket," no " bucket," their wants will supply ;
A trough they shall have in the twink of an eye ;
And while the glad sun on our efforts shall beam,
Our horses shall share in the health-giving stream.

We care little or nought for *T.C.'s gerrymanders,
And we don't fear in Vectis contagion from glanders ;
Not to drink to excess we all pledge ourselves ; stuff !
'Tis the bipeds know not when they've had quite enough.

'Twas Miss Parker who first drew men's eyes to us mokes ;
Our sufferings in summer she saw were no jokes:
And all Ventnor through centuries long shall proclaim
How our trough-donor, Livesay, hath earned him a name.

Then sound the loud timbrel o'er Ventnor's blue sea !
The Donkeys have triumphed, the mokes they are free !

---

*" Town Council." When these lines were penned, the poor mokes had not heard the good news that our Town Council had resolved to gratify their wishes. or that Mr. Livesay had kindly promised to give a site for the trough if necessary. (In the end Mr. Livesay gave the site, and laid on the water).

They are free, they are free! they shall drink of the rill
That bubbles and leaps down the side of our hill—
Our shadeless and broiling-hot Battery Hill.
May, 1894.

THE OLD ELM TREE AT ST. CATHARINE'S.

   Spare woodman! spare that old elm tree!
      Ventnor sure scarcely boasts too many.
   Each tree in Ventnor boasts its charm;—
   Spare it! if left 'twill cause no harm,
      I'll bet a sovereign to a penny.

   Sure, when a tree like that is felled,
      'Tis not an easy task to match it:
   But if it must be sacrificed,
   Town Conncillors! be well advised,
      And borrow Mr. Gladstone's hatchet!

THREE RIVAL BANDS.

Three bands in three far distant places born,
Most kindly play about our pier forlorn;
One from the town, one from the volunteers,
The third " of German origin " appears.
Play one, play all, on Esplanade or Pier,
But choose your times, so that we all may hear,
And that your townsmen peacefully may sup.
Take each your turn, and patch your squabbles up.
Three concords played at once sad discord bring;
We'll find the cash if *ye in turn* will sing;
So choose a night apiece, my worthy brother;
'Tis one good turn—not three—deserves another.

SHANKLIN v. VENTNOR.

A DIFFERENCE.

They say that in Wilts you may pass in a walk
From the " cheese " of the south to the north range
    of " chalk " ;
In our Undercliff would you a difference seek ?
Well, at Shanklin all 's Chine, and at Ventnor all
    Cheek.

"THE TWA DOGS."

I must tell you, dear Fred, how one Sunday in Lent,
Two dogs entered St. Wilfrid's, on mischief intent,
And inside the Church-porch each wicked young
    zany
(Like two quarrelsome parties, perhaps like too
    many)
Fell straight on his enemy, " hammer and tongs,"
Though they prated, like Christians, of " rights "
    and of " wrongs."
" As cool as a cucumber," good father D.,
(He 's no earthly objection to quarrels, not he !)
Quite calmly stood by, and his eyes opened wide,
Resolved in this strife not to champion one side,
But smiled sweetly on, and serenely instead,
Like Lord Burleigh, look'd wise, and just shook his
    grey head.
Still like two brave knights or belligerent yeomen
The dogs fought and tussled, each biting his foeman ;
Then awed by a sight of the whip, both the terriers
Remorseful sat quietly down on their *derriers*,
And ashamed of their wounds, though all dripping
    with gore,
Both resolved, like wise doggies, to quarrel no more.

And as for myself, I this battle rehearse,
Not in spiteful plain prose, but in humorous verse,
Content if it teaches plain Christians (like me)
From all strifes and quarrels to keep themselves free.

ANOTHER VERSION, AFTER COWPER.

'Twas early on a Sunday morn,
   Two dogs, on mischief bent,
Met at St. Wilfrid's door and growl'd,
   And bark'd with fierce intent ;

And snarl'd and bit, and bit and snarl'd,
   And made a fearful noise,
Like two fierce full-grown Christian men,
   Or two fierce Christian boys.

The congregation, panic-struck,
   Looked on in helpless fright ;
With terror grew the ladies pale,
   And screamed, as well they might.

To separate the struggling brutes
   Was not an easy matter:
We caught " Bob " by the foremost end
   And " Cæsar " by the latter.

" Bob " kept his hold, and " Cæsar " too
   To leave his grip was loth ;
Peace was at length restored when John
   Applied his whip to both.

Returning home, the dogs they mused,—
   " What sad fools are we two !
Though, after all, what have we done
   But Christians daily do ?

" Yes ! Christians of the self-same fold
   Let their fierce passions rise,
And school their tongues, if not their hands,

To tear each other's eyes.

"But we will make a truce, for fear
  Of what must follow next,
For Father D. will surely preach,
  And take *us* for his text.

"Then *shan't* we feel ashamed to be
  Held up to public scorn
For having fought our quarrel out
  On this sweet Sunday morn?"

EIDER AND EIDER-DOWN.

C—— and his wife have surely aims diverse,
  'Tis said, in whispers, throughout half the town;
The Captain strangely wants *his* Eider up,
  She no less strangely wants *her* Eider-down.

MY LATEST DREAM.

The clock had struck one, and I dozed on my bed,
And a thousand strange fancies crept into my head;
For I thought through a close iron grating I gazed
Down into H——'s dungeons, awake and amazed.
And I saw my old enemy, Peter Maguire,
Bound fast on a spit in the front of a fire
Which king Pluto had ordered his valet to light,
As " he'd asked a few friends down to supper that
    night."
I hated Maguire as fierce as could be,
(Ananias I called him) and *he* hated *me*.
And it joyed me to witness the tyrant so black
On the grin as they basted his legs and his back,
In front of the fire a-grizzling, and then
Rubbed him down with fresh mustard and *poivre
    de cayenne*.

I quickly stepped forward and said with much glee,
" I beg you, sir King, hand him over to me ;
" I'll deluge with paraffin oil the old liar
" Ananias, as if he were only a friar :
" Let me do it at once."—But just then I awoke :
His Tartarean Majesty flew off in smoke ;
And on rising I found that my dream was a joke.

ON THE DEATH OF MRS. JUDD.
JULY 6TH, 1893.

Stretched on her dying couch the mother lay,
While all the glad town smiled with garlands gay ;
Forgetting self and selfish cares, she cried
" Blithe be the children's feast " ! then calmly died.
Prayed she for others with her latest breath,
And thus disarm'd the iron hand of death.

ON THE PORTRAIT OF THE LATE A. H. HASSALL, Esq., M.D.

UNVEILED BY SIR RICHARD AND MISS WEBSTER, IN THE DINING HALL OF THE HOSPITAL FOR CONSUMPTION, AT VENTNOR, *October*, 1894.

" *Non omnis moriar*," wrote the Latin sage—
Words that will live to many a distant age.
" *Non omnis moriar*," write we 'neath the face
Of him who laboured in this pleasant place
To plant a home for sickness, and to show
How love can lighten weary weights of woe,
And, pointing onward to a brighter day,
Soothe the sad pillow of young life's decay.
Yes ! not alone in pictured form lives he.
Shrin'd in our grateful hearts his memory.

FINIS.

www.ingramcontent.com/pod-product-compliance
Lightning Source LLC
Chambersburg PA
CBHW031440160426
43195CB00010BB/798